How to
Women

The Science of Seduction

Ed West

summersdale

HOW TO PULL WOMEN

Summersdale Publishers Ltd
46 West Street
Chichester
West Sussex
PO19 1RP
UK

www.summersdale.com

Printed and bound in Great Britain

ISBN: 1-84024-545-X
ISBN: 978-1-84024-545-5

How to Pull
Women

Ed West

Contents

Introduction   7
1. My Mate Fancies You   9
2. The Evolution of Pulling   17
3. Getting Match Fit   24
4. He Who Dares Wins   31
5. How to Overcome Fear and Love Rejection   39
6. How to Meet Women   50
7. First Contact   62
8. Pack Hunting   73
9. Boy Band Theory – How to Specialise   80
10. Mistakes We Make   96
11. How to Pull Her In   114
12. How to Flirt and Compliment   124
13. Body Language   130
14. Tricks   142
15. Niche Markets   154
16. Making a Move   165
17. The Morning After   179

Introduction

Imagine learning to drive a car that had enough room for an instructor on either side. An impractical situation for our already clogged-up traffic network, but picture it anyway. Whenever your left-hand instructor said push the brake, the other told you to hit the accelerator; when one said turn left at the traffic lights, the other said go straight ahead. You'd probably be lucky to pass your test after several hundred lessons, if you hadn't by that time just given up and bought a bike.

Yet from an early age that is exactly how we are taught to attract women, despite the fact that finding a mate is far more biologically important than learning to drive, succeeding in college or buying a good house. In fact pretty much everything we do, from looking through the jobs page to saving up for a decent motor, is ultimately geared towards attracting women. What would be the point of climbing Everest or playing for England if we couldn't use it to pull women or, if we're attached, earn the love and respect of our girlfriends (and also have other women swoon when we walk past)? Men might strive for many reasons, but the underlying psychological reason is to impress women.

Like many of you, I learned the rules of attraction with two different sets of teachers – on the one hand the school of 'just be nice', and on the other the academy of 'treat 'em mean, keep 'em keen' – telling me confusing and contradictory things, and I often went wrong. I can't pretend to be a player or a stud but I've certainly learned how not to pull over the years.

I also spent several years working for men's magazines *Front* and *Nuts*, where the biggest single question asked by readers and answered by the models we interviewed was: how can a man get a woman into bed? It's not enough to say 'make 'em laugh' or 'earn loads of money', because plenty of funny blokes have no success, and becoming rich is a lot harder than chatting up a woman.

If you want words of wisdom from alpha male types who've claimed to have slept with hundreds of beautiful women, this is not for you; ditto if you want to trick women into sleeping with you – for every one that falls for it, 100 will think you're a git. If anything, you'll have to fool yourself, not women, if you want to increase your success rates. So, to think of this again as learning to drive a car: look at me as your instructor along the way, a rambling, slightly weird-looking guide who smells suspiciously of drink, but who will make you pass the test nonetheless.

You weren't born with the ability to drive a car, work a computer or speak a language – these were all taught. And it's exactly the same with attracting women – learn the right way to do it, and you'll be doing just as well as any supposed natural.

1

My Mate Fancies You

Finding one good woman, or several average ones (to borrow a line from the late Bill Hicks), is without doubt the most important thing in life, yet we never get any formal training. Our parents, while pleased if we showed interest in girls, were unlikely to encourage us too much for fear of finding something on their doorstep nine months later; our friends and older brothers offered advice that was useless, counter-productive and filled with myths likely to put us off sex for good; while we could hardly expect our over-stretched education system to teach pulling skills.

Pulling for beginners

Like men everywhere, my introduction to the mating game was a messy affair consisting of hanging around shopping centres, occasionally drinking Thunderbird, and getting a friend to say 'my mate fancies you' because I couldn't speak female.

Some people are just born with a steely nerve; the rest of us have to work on it. I could never believe the sheer balls of some of my classmates in approaching girls, especially when the corniest of lines seemed to get a result. Of course women become more sophisticated as they get older so you have to grow up with them, but the basic lesson is there. Go forth with confidence, and ye shall succeed.

Mixed messages

The major problem was, and still is, that we receive very mixed messages about how to behave in front of women. From our early teens, any woman who takes the time to speak to us will say, 'Be sensitive, but not soppy,' and 'Be manly, but not macho.' Looking at women's magazines, you'd only discover that their idea of the ideal man seemed to change from month to month.

It's confusing, and because men are single-minded and good at following instructions, we're baffled by subtleties and nuances. The things we learn in life – how machines work, the rules of sports and the basics of handling money – all have simple guidelines. If everything in life were as complex as women's hearts and loins, we'd never get anything done.

I was always told that if I just acted nice, was polite and treated them like equals, they would date me out of gratitude as much as anything else; and yet I would always be disappointed when the girls I liked ended up in the arms of the biggest dickheads in the school.

Some blokes gain some success by becoming a total bastard, and it works some of the time, and with some girls, but bastards don't just leave a trail of embittered ex-girlfriend's behind: they usually end up with no male friends, and who wants that?

Myth busting

First and foremost, let's deal with some of the myths that make their way into our heads from an early age.

You have to be a wimp or a 'lad'

Firstly, ignore the fads of the day. I spent over five years in men's magazines where other journalists often asked us to comment on cultural trends like the 'new man' or 'new lad', which were apparently types of men that emerged in the 1990s in reaction to feminism. There never was any such thing. Think about this: feminism and its demand for a more sensitive 'new' man have been around for less than 50 years; whereas the female mind has been virtually unaltered since humans came down from the trees. There is no way that a few culture shifts, or some magazines like *Cosmopolitan* or *Loaded*, are ever going to change the way that men and women feel about each other: these things are hardwired into us as much as a love of food or fear of death.

The new man and new lad have always been with us in various forms; ancient literature is filled with stories of men who either loved and cared for their families, or spent all their time getting pissed and chasing skirt. So forget being a new lad or a new man: just be a man. And before you think that's an excuse to climb back up the tree and throw empty cans of Stella from it, real men put the toilet seat down and clean up stubble hair from the sink, they just don't cry while doing so.

Men are obsolete

Then there is the myth that we are no longer needed. It is true that heavy industry has declined and that the bulk of our economy now relies on jobs that are better suited to women than those that rely on brawn. And it is also the case that fertility technology has come so far that women can become pregnant with only a test tube and a handful of sperm (so to speak), so maybe the world could largely function without men (although artificial insemination was invented by a man, and a priest to boot, way back in the late 18th century). Hospitals already have enough sperm (which can still work thousands of years after being frozen) to populate the entire galaxy.

But that's not the point. Most women wouldn't

want to live in a man-free world any more than you'd want to spend the rest of your life in a Turkish prison. Whatever their financial muscle or DIY abilities, 99 per cent of women still want a man to hold in bed and share their magic moments with. That figure, by the way, is backed up by biology: roughly one per cent of women are lesbians, while four per cent of men are gay, which means that we are technically more popular than they are.

Women go for bad boys

This is true, to an extent. Just as you want a girl who will be a whore in the bedroom but a virgin princess when meeting your parents, women want the fun and excitement of a bad boy, but without the hassle of bailing him out of jail. So they really want a good boy who can act bad when they want it.

Money and looks are what matters

You sometimes hear men label some women as gold diggers because they would go out with an elephantiasis sufferer if he drove a BMW, but what is strange is that these complaints usually come from the same men who pick women on looks. What did you expect, you idiots? A woman who looks for a rich man is just following her instinct in exactly the same way as a man who goes for a curvy bum or a great pair. His money will make sure she, and any of her offspring, are wealthy enough not to starve. Apemen several millions of years back were wooing mates by bringing back bits of meat – the convertibles of their time.

In the same way, most men are drawn to curvy figures, symmetrical faces and even blonde hair because they all suggest a woman who is healthy and able to breed, even if getting her pregnant is the last thing on their minds.

Of course if you have money women will find you attractive, but it's not just the money that is sexy. Women admire ambition and drive, and unless you got your money from a trust fund or the Lotto, it shows you're not the type of man to lie on the sofa all weekend (having said that, if you do win the Lotto you probably can expect your success rate to go up).

Women don't like sex

Women enjoy and want sex, just not necessarily with you. Women also like it in a different way to men. Their sex drive is far more complex, and emotional, which is why they are far more choosy about who they do it with. If you ever look at erotic literature and books about women's fantasies, they're incredibly detailed; men just get turned on looking at flesh, and if there were a book of our fantasies, it would have very short paragraphs. Yeah, so I gave her one, then England won the World Cup. Brilliant.

As the comedian Billy Crystal once put it: women need a reason to have sex, men just need a place. For biological reasons they need to be picky, because women can only bear one child at a time while men can (and many have) fathered dozens at the same time – and never mind that this is the 21st century, because men and women's sexual minds date back to a time when talk about social security numbers and free housing would be met with a baffled grunt. But men often make the mistake of confusing pickiness with seeing sex as a reward for our buying things or making them laugh. Never approach a woman with the mentality that you're buying her, and don't offer gifts or dinner as a down payment, because this will look like you're trying to buy her, and no woman wants to be seen as a whore, even a very pampered one.

Why do men and women have such different attitudes to procreation? Why can't we just approach a girl and say, 'Fancy a quick one?' It would work for us, after all, and we could avoid a lot of needless psychological games that cost time and money. In the human subconscious, sex leads to babies, and babies need to be looked after, and they need to be strong. Which is why women will only want to have sex with a man who will give her healthy, strong offspring, but not do a runner. From an evolutionary point of view, a gibbering drunk in a club who's unable to string a coherent sentence together unless it involves the subject of Arsenal Football Club does not appeal as a prospective mate. Women go for quality, men for quantity; a promiscuous woman is a slag, a promiscuous man is a stud. It's unfair to women who've been labelled with cruel words, but no one ever said the mating game was fair.

And just be glad you're human, since female humans are one of only two species that scientists believe actually enjoy sex (dolphins are the other, which may explain why they're always smiling). The male cat's penis has backward-pointing barbs that scrape the female upon withdrawal, while anyone who has ever heard foxes mate will know that the earth might be moving for the vixen, but she sure isn't enjoying it.

2

The Evolution of Pulling

Sexual chemistry is a misleading term, because it's more to do with biology – remember that despite the fact you wear clothes and live in a house, you are basically an ape. Everything that attracts us, both as men and women, does so because our ape-brain tells us so. The things we notice in women, and they in us, are the same things that attracted our hairy forefathers in the Stone Age; every attractive trait, whether it's in a man in uniform with bar presence, or in a fop who can recite poetry, is there because it triggers some internal mental tick.

Programmed to pull

Human society as we know it, with cities, laws, hair care products and all the other things that make us better company than gorillas, has existed for about 5,000 years; the idea of marrying for love is less than 700 years old; modern contraceptive methods less than 50 years old. The human mind, in its current form, is at least a quarter of a million years old, and much of it has remained unchanged since as far back as three million years ago, when our ancestors became the upwardly mobile branch of the primate family, and became too embarrassed to invite their chimp relatives over for Christmas any more. Homo sapiens date from between 140,000 to 500,000 years ago, but it depends on your definition of human. Some argue that the earlier evolutionary stages of man weren't entirely human, but while we can never know what they thought of life, looks-wise you could put them in a suit and stick them outside a nightclub and no one would be any the wiser.

No wonder then that the current rules for courtship – monogamous marriage, no kissing until the third date, being a 'nice guy' – are up against ingrained sexual programming more suited towards life in the stone age savannah than the office. Every single heterosexual man and woman on the planet has a pre-written Post-it note in their mind that tells them to look for someone to mate with. Every time an available woman gets dressed for the evening, every time she surveys a room in a party, and every time she asks, 'So what do you do?', she is subconsciously assessing you as a potential mate. Even when your girlfriend asks about your family she is slyly assessing your family for signs of genetic faults.

The bad news is this is often done in nanoseconds; when a woman glances at you and then never looks back, her mating mind has assessed and rejected you. Too short, too fat, too ruddy-faced? I don't want my children looking like that.

Men with symmetrical faces, which indicate health, also begin with a couple of aces in their pack; and features like big eyes, healthy skin and well-toned muscles also help.

Height is important, indicating strength and an ability to lord it over other men (tall men earn far more than short men, in every country on earth). Being able to protect a woman from other men is a great asset, and women who've experienced violence are more likely to plump for goliaths. Of course, even if you're a gentle giant and incapable of making money it won't really matter, because the advantage is still there, and at the very least you'll be able to put your woman on your shoulders at a gig.

But height can be compensated for with personality; often when meeting very charismatic men people are surprised to find out just how short they are, and it's not because they're wearing high heels – their personalities are worth an extra couple of inches. Why? Because something happened when the apemen of the Miocene era looked around and thought, 'You know, there's got to be more to life than climbing up trees and picking nits out of each other's hair.' We started talking. And the vast majority of female attraction is not about what we look like, but what we say. Luckily when our ancestors went one way and the chimps went the other, we were given the chance to redeem all our misfortune with the gift of the gab – we call it charm.

Charm the pants off

What is charm? Charm is a social skill that allows us to get our way with people, to make friends, and establish a decent place in the pecking order without physical strength or money, but through wit, courtesy and a certain charisma. Charm can be learned but it can't be faked, which is why when a salesman does it wrong we think they're being smarmy and disgusting. If you look at the great charmers from movie history (although I think Face from *The A-Team* was the ultimate example), they were complimentary, generous in spirit, welcoming, always polite, and they made other people feel comfortable and safe. Such a skill is so important to us because humans live in such large groups and charm goes a long, long way. So if you're able to charm a woman, she'll know you'll be able to charm her family, the man at the restaurant who deals with table bookings, and future employers. Charm = success.

And charm also makes a woman feel good about herself. Even the most stunning women on earth need to feel good, just as we do, and so men who can pull this off will never find themselves alone at night subscribing to Playboy TV.

Because charming people seem so effortlessly comfortable in company, we tend to associate charm with another great quality – confidence, by far the most important asset of all. Once you develop charm, your confidence levels will go through the roof as you realise how easy it is to get your way.

It doesn't matter how funny, rich or good-looking you are: if you have no faith in yourself and your worth, a woman won't want to know. Confidence is a self-fulfilling prophecy, and confident people try and try again until eventually they succeed. Why else would the self-help sector of the book trade be so big? Look on Amazon.com to see how many books have been published teaching people to believe in themselves. Whatever you say about Americans, they certainly don't lack confidence, and their economy reflects this.

Practise developing your charm with everyone you speak to, not just women.

- When a woman from a call centre says 'Hi, my name's Katie' in that overly friendly manner they're forced to adopt, reply 'Hi Katie' and be polite and generous, complimenting her on how well she treated you (even if you want to slam the phone down or shout, 'Stop calling me, you evil scum!')

- When you next ring a builder or plumber, try to haggle the price down ten per cent, and

when they say no (as they will 95 per cent of
the time), be perfectly polite and charming.

- Go into an emptyish pub and ask if you can use
  the toilet. If you're polite and charming, they
  will let you.

- If there's someone difficult at work, see if you can
  get a smile out of them.

All of these things might seem irrelevant to pulling, but
they're useful exercises for developing your charm.

Quantity v quality – men and women and sex

Women are fussy with their choice of sexual partner,
while most men, as we all know, will cheerfully
couple with anything with a backbone, especially if
drink is involved. Why? As with all mammals, male
humans are far more diverse than the female, in that
the difference between the most and least intelligent
men is greater than with women (one test, of 80,000
Scottish children, found that there were 15 per cent
more male geniuses, but also 17 per cent more male
thickos). No wonder then that in most species, a tiny
proportion of the males mate with all the females; in
elephant seal societies, one male out of a couple of
hundred may get 80 per cent of all the sex (imagine
how much the others must hate his guts).

It also happens in the human world: Mongol warlord Genghis Khan, who shagged his way through Asia in the 14th century, has around 17 million descendants today, including the royal families of Britain and Iran (and you may be one), while his followers had to console themselves with, at best, his sloppy seconds, while a recent DNA test showed that two per cent of New Yorkers were descended from one very horny medieval Irish chieftain called Brian, a clan leader who took all the girls for himself. But it doesn't mean that every time you go to Yates's Wine Lodge you should act like Genghis Khan – you'd probably get glassed, and certainly arrested – because times have changed and today's leaders don't grab all the nation's women for themselves (it would be really bad for the opinion polls).

But in order to attract women, you have to give the appearance that you're the alpha male – in other words, show that you're a leader, not a follower. And doing that is not at all difficult, it's just that some men have worked it out and some haven't.

3

Getting Match Fit

Some of you might be new to the game, some maybe out of practice, while others are just keen to try new tactics. But whether it's learning something new or conquering a phobia (and pulling brings its fair share of those), the key is practice and experience. If you do it enough, you'll get better and lose all those worries. How hard can it be, after all? To come back to the driving metaphor, there are plenty of thick blokes out there succeeding, so there's no reason for you to fail.

If you have been out of the game for a while, you've probably become slouchy, fat and lazy about your appearance. This is the first thing to sort out, because it's the easiest. A makeover (I hate the term, but I'm afraid they're yet to think of a more blokey word for it) will make you look more attractive to the opposite sex, and far more importantly, give you extra confidence.

Firstly, the gym

There's something about going to the gym that is narcissistic, shallow and, well, a bit poncy, but it does the job; alternatively if you have mates to play football, squash or badminton with, do that instead, but twice a week is the minimum. Or just buy a bike and save money on fares or petrol.

There's no need to go for big muscles or a six-pack, but excess fat is easily removed with the occasional go on the treadmill. Women like a man with strong shoulders, so work on these moderately, and likewise with your biceps. But most important of all is the stomach. Women always look at the long-term prospect of a man, so if he has a belly in his twenties, imagine what a useless slovenly lump he'll be in ten years time. So if you do any muscle work at all, then, use the Abdominizer, or whatever the hell it's called. Giving up the beer for a couple of weeks will also work wonders.

Regular exercise also lifts our mood, because it releases endorphins into the bloodstream, the happy hormones most famously found in Ecstasy. So next time someone in a club asks if you have any pills, tell them in your best sergeant major's voice to take a run around the block.

After a couple of weeks in the gym, you'll feel better, happier and sexier, and will find the women who work at the gym smiling your way a lot more, or at the very least not looking at you like they've just seen your face on the front cover of the News of the World. Some seduction guides even suggest chatting up women in between working out, but I'd be cautious. None of us look very dignified wheezing away after a knackering 1.5 kilometre run, and women feel just as self-conscious, especially as it's the one place where they're scantily clad for the sole reason that there's no alternative. So my advice is, if you do start talking to them, make it jokey and equipment-related to start with, and see how it progresses. But in any case you'll get to meet women, and if it's near to your local pub, you'll be able to start conversations with fellow gymsters there.

Clothes

Good clothes certainly help, but more important is the fact that dressing well gives you far more confidence. In other words, it's psychosomatic – you'll feel more attractive, and so will become more attractive.

If you have a female friend, and you're uncertain of your look, get her to dress you. She'll probably jump at the chance to make you her project, you'll get a look designed towards women, and the girls in the shops will love you for being so open to female influence.

Women love to change a man, and since they're very unsuccessful in getting us to stop boozing or making our toilet habits less repulsive, changing our wardrobe is a rare victory.

Otherwise there are many varying styles, but the golden rule is to be yourself, at least to start with. Some people can pull off a white suit because they have the confidence (or arrogance); for the rest of us, simply looking smart is probably the best we can hope for.

Among 'pick-up artists', the American term for men who have mastered the art of attracting women, there is a concept known as peacock theory, which holds that wearing extravagant clothes such as an outlandish hat, chain mail or having black painted nails is the key to attracting a woman. But bear in mind this theory came out of California, where such behaviour is part of the culture; in most of Britain, you'd probably just get your head kicked in.

On the other hand, do wear something that's a conversational piece or indicates you've done something interesting, such as a ring, strange watch or shark's tooth. Even better if it has a fascinating story behind it, or you can make one up easily.

And avoid dressing down in order to get that 'slacker' look: rock stars can get away with it because they're on stage; other men just look like tramps. While you can look good in a plain T-shirt and jeans if the setting is right, make sure they're ultra-clean. You wouldn't turn up to face a potential employer or a judge looking like a hobo, so why should the first time you meet the potential woman of your dreams be any different?

Male grooming

Smell plays an enormous part in mating, up to 10 per cent in some studies. Ever been with a girl who wasn't amazing looking but just smelled right? Your nose glands are giving you a signal that she is a suitable mate, and her scent glands – pheromones – are working on you. Of course your nose glands aren't the ones that have to put up with her tantrums and *Celebrity Love Island* chit-chat, which is why they're only allowed a minority vote.

Remembering how important smell is in attraction, aftershave gives you a clear advantage in the mating stakes, but don't overdo it. A couple of squirts onto the wrists and then dabbed on the neck is enough, or spray some at head level and walk into it. There are a variety of aftershaves on offer, so it's difficult to single out one, but Prada and Gucci are both popular with the ladies. While I was at *Front* we held a test where four glamour models judged various scents on Britain's premier Asian dwarf Elvis impersonator, and I seem to remember Hugo Boss came off best, but you may disagree. Always ask women their opinion on your aftershaves when the opportunity arises, as some scents will suit your natural odour better than others.

Alternatively, try spreading the scent of cucumber and liquorice together on your neck, by crushing them into a paste. This might sound a bit extreme, but a study by Chicago University found that the scent of these two products increased blood flow to the vagina by 13 per cent, whereas expensive colognes had no or negative impact. Also popular was baby powder (13 per cent) and lavender and pumpkin pie mixed together (11 per cent) – God knows why they stumbled upon this combination. The least sexy smell was charred barbecued meat.

Always put a small amount of wax or gel in your hair; always make sure you've cleaned around your armpits, face and nether regions; moisturise as much as possible to keep your skin fresh; and learn as much as you can about grooming in general. I had a friend who worked at a beauty salon and his ability to advise women about which moisturiser or foundation suited them best, when all the other blokes were talking about car engines, put him head and shoulders above the rest. Speaking of which, make sure you don't have dandruff.

If you're in doubt about shaving and strange body hair, just shave it off. If in doubt about anything, go with the majority, unless you have total belief in a certain look. Have you ever noticed how people with dyed pink hair and nose rings tend to be quite boring? Let your mouth make statements, not your look. For more on male grooming, I've written a book called, of all things, *Male Grooming*, which you'll find at most good bookshops.

Haircut

Most men still like to go a bloke's barber shop where, for £6, a man will give you a grade four while talking about football in an overly masculine way, as if he's desperate that you don't think he's gay. I happen to think there's something weird about the way women can spend £75 on a haircut (never mind feeding a starving third world family, they could fly the lot over here for lunch). But just this once, go and spend £25 on a proper haircut in a unisex salon. No man will notice the difference, but women definitely will. Even going into those places gives you a confidence boost; if you get your hair done by a female hairdresser, chances are she'll be stunning and, perhaps thinking you're a successful metrosexual kind of guy, will smile and laugh at all your lame jokes.

Teeth

Likewise, get your teeth properly cleaned at a private dental surgery. An hour's job will cost up to £80 (or half that for half an hour), but you'll notice one hell of a difference. Bad teeth are one of those things women notice much more than men, and you'll probably also rid yourself of another silent passion-killer: bad breath.

On a final note: get a decent pair of shoes. For some unknown reason, women place huge emphasis on shoes, and even the greatest biologists in the land haven't got a clue why.

4

He Who Dares Wins

OK, so you probably shouldn't think about pulling women in terms of being an SAS soldier, but their motto is appropriate enough. Confidence is by far the most important secret to a seducer's success. You can be ugly, short, boring and skint, but if you know what you want, and in your head you're good enough, you can pull almost any woman. I've known so many blokes in this category who have walked off with the girl – often the girl I was umming and arring to only an hour before, not doing anything especially wrong except showing a lack of belief in myself.

Of course, confidence is one of those things you either have or you haven't, right? Not at all – as I mentioned earlier, there is a substantial market in selling confidence, with books with titles like *Unleash the Warrior Within*, *How To Win Friends and Influence People*, and *Don't Just Stand There You F★★★ing Idiot, Do Something With Your Life*.

Because no one is simply born with confidence. Some develop it from an early age but most learn it themselves, and this is where reading about it can be very useful. Confidence is about knowledge, because that is what defeats fear. When we overcome fear, it's only because we have learned that there is nothing to be afraid of.

People can lose their confidence as well as gaining it, and like a house of cards it can be smashed to pieces by traumatic events of a harsh dumping – the test is to get over those setbacks and walk up to the next woman.

Sophie Howard

Readers of *Nuts* and other men's magazines will be acquainted with Sophie Howard, one of the best-paid models in the country. This is how Sophie recommends you impress her:

'I have been blown away by confidence. There's a guy I knew who was so confident, and I didn't really know why. And it just made me believe it. But you have to know that fine line between confident and arrogant: have inner confidence, be confident within yourself. And how do you get it? You pretend. Girls pretend to be sexy, and you guys fall for it.'

You're the prize

Many men make the mistake of thinking that attraction, or seduction, is about tricking women into buying a dud – i.e. themselves. Think like that and you're bound to come across as shifty and sly, when in fact what you should be selling is a great time, interesting conversation and presumably a sexual rollercoaster (or at least a dodgem). It's a two way thing, remember; you're both after the same thing, just trying to work out with whom.

A man with a plan

You have to know what you want from life. What career do you want, how do you expect to pay a mortgage? Do you have a fantastic ambition, and do you have a sensible Plan B ready if it doesn't work? What's your plan? Women love a man with a plan, and that goes even for fairly unrealistic ones. I've known one or two men who've kept hold of girlfriends despite years of sponging because they've always got a new get-rich-quick scheme up their sleeve. Women love the idea of a man who's going to reach the top from the bottom, especially if they can be the other half of the power couple (they'd also be given half of it in a divorce court, which helps).

Take your lead from the world of self-help and think like a Yank. They didn't just sit in their gardens looking at the Moon; they hired some Nazi scientists and invaded the bastard. So tell the next girl you meet that your ambition is to be an astronaut. The worst that will happen is she'll laugh.

Be busy

Nothing destroys your confidence with women more than sitting around moping about the fact you have no confidence with women. Buy a small appointments diary, and keep it filled. Make sure you're always busy socialising, working or even doing evening classes. Anything from languages to cooking classes; they'll all improve your pulling skills, not to mention introduce you to loads of girls. Any venue that is vaguely self-improving, from the library to first aid courses, will be about three-quarters female – you can either take this as depressing proof that we're doomed as a sex, or be thankful that the competition is so useless. A busy man is an attractive man, and wallowing will kill you if you let it. But don't take so many jobs that you don't have time to go out, obviously.

Sarah from Derbyshire says:
'I did a foreign language class and there were three guys and 18 girls. They had such a good time, and after each class some of us would go out for drinks; we used to swarm around them, poor things!'

Act attached

Think like a man in a relationship, and act like you have a girlfriend. You don't have to buy a ring for yourself, but one of the annoying things about life is that women find you far more attractive when you're hooked up already. Attached men have a certain carefree air that is the opposite of the tongue hanging out, 'please have sex with me' look of the long-term single desperado. Go to pubs with a female friend, or other places where women will see you. They'll talk to you far more, and you'll feel less like a man with an extensive DVD 'art house' collection.

That's mainly because women will feel safe around you if they don't think you're on the lookout like some sex-starved meerkat, and less suspicious of your 'accidental' brush against their breast. In this way you end up in the brilliant position of being able to show your sexuality by smiling and flirting, but while not being a threat.

Presentation

Don't mumble. In extreme cases you can even see a therapist, but practise speaking clearly and confidently, and don't let your voice trail off as if even you don't care what you're saying. If you're really concerned, buy a Dictaphone and listen to yourself; it's cringe-worthy, but anything that makes you cringe only makes you stronger and ballsier.

Successful ladies' men all learn to ignore embarrassment and develop superbug-like resistance to it.

And if you're smiling and positive, and generous with your compliments, people will be attracted to you. Research has shown that, not only is yawning addictive, but so is happiness and goodwill; *Emotional Contagion*, written by two shrinks and a historian, found that happy people cause others to feel happy around them. That's why we feel some have a natural aura, and almost feel addicted to them.

Stance

The biggest stud in my school wasn't the best looking or smartest, but he was the only one who didn't walk around with a Generation X slouch. He strolled with broad shoulders, and when he stepped into the room women knew that here was a man who believed in his own worth. Like many people in their twenties, I'm now trying to correct a lifetime's slouching. Not only is it a huge disadvantage in the workplace, where arse-kicking corporate types see it as a sign of laziness and weakness, but it can lead to all sorts of back problems in later life, not to mention signalling to any attentive women that here is a man who would rather be playing video games at home than carrying her up a flight of stairs, fireman-style, for a night of passion.

You can help things by signing up to an Alexander technique class, which will correct bad posture. And, yes, you will probably be the only man in the class. Otherwise, simple back exercises will get you standing tall.

And it's not just stance – you have to walk like a man as well, making strong, purposeful strides. Think of The Fonz, Arnie and Russell Crowe rolled into one.

And hold your head up high!

Hollie from Telford

'I got into a relationship with a man who was what I would call "magnetic". He wasn't good-looking but was very career minded, sociable and didn't feel any need to impress anyone. I found this very attractive.'

Take a holiday

If your confidence needs a boost, practise with a holiday. Depending on what floats your boat, whether it's Magaluf or the ski slopes, women are much easier to talk to, and to pull, on holiday. The social pressures that keep women from being more forward back home – the fear of getting a reputation as a 'slag' – disappear abroad, plus they're also feeling a lot better and therefore a lot sexier themselves. Perhaps it's the booze, sun or congregation of lots of young people all with the same thing on their mind, but most women are up for a fling. Remember Eddie Murphy's joke about how women lie about how many men they've slept with, that they don't count holiday flings, only 'domestic dick'. It's a different world, and many women who wouldn't look your way in Britain will sleep with you in Spain.

Anthropologists call it 'cultural remission', an area where

normal social rules are relaxed. Women at the New Orleans Mardi Gras will expose themselves in exchange for beads, but wouldn't really consider doing the same at work.

Be playful

Before going somewhere where you'll meet women, watch a comedy, think about your favourite lines from *The Simpsons*, and put a smile on your face. Think like a bubbly, lively, funny and confident person from the TV. Alternatively, and I'm not joking, think about being a puppy. Puppies are playful, enthusiastic and friendly. Quite the opposite of the wolf, which is what we end up looking like when we leer at women like a predator.

Don't be serious; this is not the be all and end all, this is just a game. How you do at pulling, as opposed to finding the right girl when you're older, is not in any way a reflection of you any more than your ability to play pool. Besides which, once you start to pick up a bit of success you'll soon stop taking it so seriously, and as a result will be still more successful.

James from Kent

'I'm English but my family is Irish, and when I go out to pull I imagine I'm Irish (without actually putting the accent on), because I associate being Irish with being jolly, good fun and up for a laugh. Playful, in other words. I also passed my driving test on the third go after hitting on the same idea, but this time imagining in my head that I'm German. Sounds mental, but it worked.'

5

How to Overcome Fear and Love Rejection

'Go up to her, what are you afraid of?' is the catchphrase of the little voice inside us, but we all know that what we fear is rejection. It's such a cruel word that some of us can't even bear to say it.

There is a theory that rejection holds this fear over us because our ancestors lived in small groups, where the whole clan would know about one knock-back, and it might damage a man's chances of mating forever. But unless you live on an island in the South Atlantic, or make your sorry pass on *Big Brother*, there's no way a few no's are going to harm you in this day and age.

The truth is nature has hardened men to rejection; women take it far worse. Those apemen whose genes survived didn't wander into the savannah to cry; they dusted themselves down, moved on and tried again. And the ultimate result of that? All of us. Remember: you have those successful mating genes in you.

I once asked a journalist who'd made a successful career in one of the most competitive industries there is how he handled the initial rejections, which can be relentless and heartbreaking. His answer? He pasted his bedroom with rejection slips. He learned to love them, because every failure taught him something and moved him closer to his goal. This is something that most American seduction gurus will tell you, indeed any self-help bloke with a name like Tiberius Cash and a giant bouffant: every failure is a lesson.

Persistence pays off, and it's exactly the same in the mating game as it is in the toughest of careers. The problem is that most of us remember the first times we were rejected by girls, usually in depressing ice-skating rinks. These blanks were often cruel, and very, very public. Often we'd be too traumatised to approach a girl for months, and I don't think anyone forgets those early setbacks.

Yet some of my schoolmates just went for it, got knocked back, and were laughed at by everyone, but in the end had the last laugh. We all laughed at the boys who got egg on their face, but only because of jealousy at their courage and determination. Eventually their persistence paid off, and they got phone numbers and maybe even a snog, or got to stick a hand up her blouse.

Of course as we get older rejection becomes less cruel, and more private, but it still hurts. So what? If you're afraid of something like that, how are you ever going to face something like your parents dying, losing your job or watching England getting knocked out by a Big Phil Scolari team? Put it in perspective.

You have to be able to laugh at the rejection, and know that if you ever meet the woman again, you could honestly smile thinking about the whole thing. The chances are that next time you meet the girl who said 'you ming' outside the multiplex, you'll be a lot richer while she'll have four kids by five different fathers, or some other horror story.

David from Walsall
'It's all about the numbers game. I have a friend who isn't particularly good with women but he just tries it on such a large number that he's pulled more than anyone. The one pull makes the dozen rejections worthwhile.'

Batting averages

And don't be put off by a low score rate, because your batting average is going to be low whatever your situation; if a man has slept with 1,000 women, the chances are he's made a pass at 10,000. You probably don't have the time or inclination to go that far, but remember that there are 3 billion women out there, and even taking away the underage, senile, married and imprisoned, in your day to day work and socialising, you're never more than about ten ft away from an eligible bachelorette.

Someone once pointed out to me that a tiger fails in 95 per cent of its hunts; ignoring the fact that it's quite a sinister analogy, you don't imagine the tiger thinks after its prey has outpaced it, 'God, I'm such a pathetic tiger, what will the other big cats think?' Perhaps a better comparison is with marketing; those annoying people who call you offering new phone deals consider it a good day if two per cent of people take up their offer. Because what we're all doing every time we approach a woman with the intention of asking her out is selling ourselves as a product (and professional salesmen, for that reason, make very good seducers).

Overcoming fear

Any self-help guide, whatever the field it covers, will tackle the problem of fear. Fear is what stops us achieving our goals, but it does have a very useful purpose, especially if our goal is to jump over a ravine on Rollerblades. But you have to differentiate between inbuilt sensible fears and irrational phobias; the fear of snakes is there for a reason – look at a baby orang-utan when its eyes first notice anything slithery and you'll know it goes way back, because the ancestors who didn't fear snakes got strangled or poisoned and didn't pass on their 'no fear' attitude. It's the same with flying: sure, your chances of crashing are a million to one at worst, but it's still perfectly rational for a human to feel uneasy six miles up in the air.

Compare these to a fear of approaching women, where the result of failure is not death but a mere slap or snigger, and most likely just a vague feeling of embarrassment and ridiculousness.

And those blokes who just go up to a woman without seeming to have a care in the world and talk to her are no different to the rest of us. They, too, feel the fear, but they turn that fear to their advantage, and like with a rollercoaster ride, use it for the adrenaline rush. Of course the more they do it, the easier it gets, so that for some men chasing women becomes the thrill in itself, to the point where it gets boring when she succumbs.

Whenever we approach a woman, these are the thoughts that come into our heads:

What if she just laughs in my face?

Forget about it, because it's sure to happen at some point, but it doesn't matter. Everyone has their insecurities, and you can be sure that the bigger the put-down, the unhappier she is with herself. Don't take it personally either; you may have just approached her at the wrong time. And sometimes, when a girl's friends say, 'She's not a bitch, she's just shy,' they mean it.

She's also got that invisible protective screening process to weed out potential timewasters; the men who don't have the right stuff and will not make the grade by turning out to be weirdos, mummy's boys or alcoholics. Don't take it personally: it's the equivalent of an employer throwing your CV on the rejection pile before you get an interview. You know you're good enough for the job, but your presentation probably needs working on.

What if I run out of things to say, or freeze?

Not a problem. If a woman doesn't respond and you don't know if you're even making sense, it doesn't really hurt to ramble on. I know a bloke who was called Mr Random by three different girls because his approach was to just talk and talk and talk, but he could always rescue the situation by saying 'sorry, I have no idea what I'm on about.' Sometimes it worked, sometimes it didn't, but he was far more successful than he would have been had he just given up and made a hasty retreat.

What if she thinks I'm a perv or a weirdo?

You mustn't forget that women are after the same thing you are, but they're just playing their role in the game. So you like sex? You're a man; don't be ashamed of it (of course if you're reading this in suspenders and a Mexican wrestling mask, maybe you should be worried).

What if she's out of my league?

Nine times out of ten it will be the man, not the woman, who rejects himself as being not good enough, especially if she's stunning in her glad rags and he's not feeling his best. By thinking that way when you approach her, you're automatically relegating yourself from her league before she's even caught your eye. In journalism one of the scariest things, in fact the scariest thing, is interviewing celebrities; at first you're just grateful to be in their presence and are ever so 'umble. Then after a couple of bad ones you end up thinking, are these people demigods? Have they cured cancer? Of course not, they're just people like the rest of us, special in some way (and often not), but still with the same weaknesses and insecurities; everyone goes to the toilet, after all. Once a journalist realises this, they become much better at interviewing. Likewise don't put women on a pedestal; they are wonderful and make life worth living, but they're your equal, not your superior, however beautiful they are.

People always tell you that when addressing an audience you should imagine them naked. It's probably not a good idea to do the same with a beautiful woman, but try picturing her at her worst; first thing in the morning, or with funny sticky-out ears, or even going to the toilet (try to remove that image once you've actually won her over and it's safe to revert to the naked image again).

Are my flies undone?
Well, best check that one before.

For all these reasons, except the last obviously, it's best to adopt the number one principle of pick-up artists: the three-second rule. Once you've made eye contact with a girl, go straight up to her before you get a chance to lose it, telling yourself that you're too busy to mess around. If you allow three seconds to pass without doing anything, your confidence, and your chances, drop dramatically. Chances are, unless you are given a chance to speak to her later, you've blown it – now move on.

The act

Men often try to overcome this fear of ridicule and rejection by putting on an act. That way, if we then get a glare or a sneer, it's not us but the persona that was rejected. Unfortunately women see through this sham, and not surprisingly it decreases your chances a whole lot more. Ask 100 women what turns them off most, and 'putting on an act' always comes up top. It's easy for professional seducing gurus to say, 'be yourself', especially when you find out a lot of them are bodybuilders or rich, but what about the rest of us? Well, the same still rings true, sort of. Women know when a man is being false, so focus on the best aspects of you and pitch yourself with these in mind.

Think about the best character traits you have, and focus on them, maximising their potential; if you're funny but cowardly, don't pretend to be a tough guy because you think it'll impress women. They'll see through it, and rather than thinking, 'He makes me laugh, I'd love to wake up with him in the morning, if only for the craic,' they'll just think, 'He's trying too hard, what a loser.' Every man in the world has at least one positive quality – use it.

How to stand your ground

All animals, including humans, are equipped with an instinctive response called 'fright, flight or fight'. It's a massive rush of adrenaline that causes us to run away or stand our ground when confronted by a threat, be it a ravenous wolf in prehistoric times, or a drunk maniac in a train station pub today. It also works the same with frightening social situations.

Pub fights generally follow a pattern: a man starts on another man, who then responds either with submission or counter-aggression, and then the aggressor moves in to attack. This might only take two or three seconds, but those few seconds can seem a long time in an intense situation; and if you've been in those situations before, you soon learn how to tell from a man's body language whether or not he's lost his bottle.

Just with making war, it's the same with making love. Though chatting up a woman is very different to starting a fight with a man, both involve the same quality: nerve, adrenaline, testosterone and a raised heartbeat, and in both cases you're out to prove that you're the dominant male. And when you walk across the bar in a matter of seconds, it's time enough for you to go from alpha male to zero.

So just remember when you make that walk: if it goes wrong, she's not going to punch you in the face. Unless, perhaps, if you live in Salford. Our fear of violence is a very real, and very useful, skill we've been handed in our genes, like a fear of heights or fire. A fear of rejection is just a neurosis. But just like with martial arts, the key to it is controlling your breathing: this controls the flow of blood to the brain that otherwise makes us panic.

Ross Jeffries, the American seduction guru who created speed seduction (see the chapter on 'Tricks'), advises us to control our breathing in this situation, by taking deep breaths through the nose, expanding the rib cage and then holding your breath briefly. This will help you deal with any nerve-wracking situation and is very effective when making that scary approach.

Michael from Yorkshire

'I used to get physically nauseous talking to girls, I was so scared, and it made me feel like a bit of a freak. Then I read something about how actors often puke before a big performance, and the best ones did it most. Now I don't feel like less of a man just because I get scared, but more because I go ahead and do it anyway.'

Training exercises

As with any phobia, the more you do it, the less frightening it becomes. So try, for instance, going up to a random woman and saying something in a matter-of-fact way, maybe paying her a compliment, making it clear you're not chatting her up, then walking off and saying 'Nice to have met you, I'll see you around.' You weren't trying to get in her pants, you're not a perv, and even if she's not interested in you, so what? You're not interested in her, so no one's a winner or loser. And it wasn't that scary, was it? If you're worried she might insult you, start your speech by saying you have to go in a couple of minutes (called a time constraint by Ross Jeffries, who we'll come to later).

One warm-up exercise advocated by seduction gurus is to go to a shopping centre and say 'Hi' to every young, attractive woman you see. Take it one step further and try getting a summer job or volunteer work that forces you to approach women, such as one of those annoying charity muggers you see everywhere. A few weeks doing that, and you'll never have the slightest fear of approaching women; in fact, trying to snog them will seem a lot easier than convincing them to donate £10 a month to some whales.

6

How to Meet Women

Befriend women

Pulling without first making friends with women is a bit like trying to get past an angry bouncer in an all-male group; you might just do it, but you're making things a great deal harder.

Women will always find it slightly strange if you don't have any female friends. Do you not enjoy their company? Are you perfectly happy to be in an all-male world all the time? Women can start to seem strange and alien if you stay away from them long enough, so make an effort.

Many of us hate the very word 'friend'; we've been given that fobbing off too many times before, the insult made all the worse by some lame explanation that we're more special because they've chosen us as a platonic buddy but find the thought of actually having sex with us disgusting. That's bullshit, because a good boyfriend is also a best friend, and would they tell Tom Cruise that if he turned up in town? 'Sorry, Tom, can I just talk to you about my ex instead, I just don't see you that way...'

But though the friend zone is a desolate monastery where we peer out of the windows to our rivals having a far better time in Boyfriend Ville or even F★★★buddy-on-sea, it has its bonuses. A female friend will do wonders for your potential with other women.

Pivots

Tony Clink, a self-proclaimed pick-up artist who wrote *The Layguide*, calls them 'pivots', and these friendly women act as a bridge between you and potential sexual partners. Your female friend, by agreeing to hang around you, has implicitly recommended you to her sisters, and at the very least they'll know you're not a serial killer. Having a drink with her will also give you the appearance of an attached man, at least on first impressions (enough to get your foot in the door). If you're with a female friend you can easily sit down at a table with two girls and start a conversation without feeling too obvious.

So befriend women, either your cousins, friends' girlfriends, colleagues or just girls next door. Your new buddy will tell you where you're going wrong; men in comparison have very shallow relationships with each other, based around trivia, common interests, and drinking, and many men can be good friends for years without having a single deep conversation, let alone waxing lyrical about the perils of love. Your female friend will tell you what clothes to wear, how to act around women (and what's a turn-off), and she may even introduce you to an available buddy.

A good pivot should be popular, outgoing, feminine, and a born matchmaker. She doesn't have to be good-looking, and she's not there as your status symbol. If she has a boyfriend, befriend him and make sure he knows you're not a threat. If she doesn't, then of course something might develop along the way.

There is one exception to the pivot rule: the girl who doesn't want you but doesn't want anyone else to have you either. If a female friend is reluctant to set you up or help you chat up girls, lay down the law and tell her that, as a friend, it's her job to help your love life, just as a male friend would.

Emily from Leeds

'Girls who want you all to themselves but only as a friend have confidence and security issues and secretly fancy you. People who are insecure seek status from the things around them – clothes, cars, haircuts, their "cool" friends, having a sexy boyfriend – whereas people who are secure just don't need those things.'

Practice makes perfect

Practise flirting in non-pulling situations when you can, such as with the check-out girl or hairdresser. Men can get out of the habit of flirting if they're in a relationship because they tend to do it as a seduction warm-up while women just flirt for fun, but it's natural and ingrained in all of us. When I say flirting I don't mean crude innuendo or lip licking; just a smile and a joke to start with. Go to beauty salons or other women's shops to buy a present for your mum or sister. The shop assistant will welcome your request for help, and will probably enjoy helping to choose a present. She'll probably wish her boyfriend were as caring as you.

Research

Get inside women's minds. Watch TV programmes that women watch. Read magazines like *Cosmopolitan* and *Glamour*, to see what women are interested in these days, whether it's the latest fashion, or sex tips. And even have a look at a romantic novel that has been a massive seller with the ladies – the lines inside are written by women who know what words turn women on.

Study the masters

Next time you're with a friend who is really good with the ladies, just sit back and watch him in action. Try to listen for what he says, watch his body language, how he addresses a group of girls and singles one out; even better if he's not very good looking and has to win them over with sheer balls (so to speak).

Work

Unless you're still in education, your workplace is your number one source of new friends and opportunities, and the most readily available supply of new women. If you're not actively seeking a career right now, look for jobs that will help you meet ladies. Big companies are better, while certain industries are far more female-friendly; anything where talking is more important than lifting things will have a decent number of women.

Fancy an office fling?

A 2003 survey by Trojan® Brand Condoms revealed the best industries for office flings.

1. Advertising/Marketing
2. Pharmaceuticals
3. Telecoms
4. Financial Services
5. Sales
6. Accountancy
7. Law
8. IT (Information Technology)
9. Broadcasting
10. Education

And here were the worst:
26. Charity
27. Internet/New Media
28. Publishing
29. Research
30. Architecture

Pubs

Only a generation ago men comprised 90 per cent of pub goers, and it was even tradition in many parts of the country for women to sit in a separate bar. What, you have to ask, was the point of going out at all?

Thankfully the whole pub-going experience has become far less of a bloke fest and the breweries, never slow to spot a money-making opportunity, have opened thousands of female-friendly bars and pubs across the country. These tend to be open-planned, filled with mirrors, comfortable sofas and other feminine fixtures and fitting. But most of all, they're clean, and a bit more expensive, of course. But despite being aimed at women, men have actually showed a preference for these more hygienic, less testosterone-charged pubs, not just because there are women, but because they found they actually preferred sofas to broken chairs with protruding nails, a good example of the civilising effect of the fairer sex.

If you're lucky enough to have a local like this, befriend the barman. If the place gets busy then a mate behind the beer pump will help no end, as bar presence is one of those strange things that people associate with dominant, charismatic men, while barmen often go on to parties after hours. In fact if you want to be a Casanova, barmen are notorious for sleeping around.

Dave from Middlesex

'My friend Rob is a normally shy person but when he's behind the bar he gets into this role, where he's friendly and smiley. His pulling rate has increased about ten-fold since he switched jobs, and it's not just that he meets some women. It's a form of continuing market research because you get to talk to hundreds, and after such a large quantity of talking and flirting, you get to see what works and what doesn't. Plus he always gets invited to parties.'

Pub feng shui

Getting there early to grab a good spot will pay dividends, but make sure it's in the cleanest place with the most light, as women will congregate in this area. Also try to position yourself next to the women's toilet; you'll find a steady conga line of females, and will be able to make an initial approach when they're on their own, rather than in a big group.

Having said that, the bar itself is the best place to start talking to anyone in the pub, let alone women. This is the public zone, where inter-stranger contact is more acceptable; approaching a woman at a table with her friends can seem like an invasion of personal space, just as we often get annoyed when charity collectors approach us for money at our tables when we're just having a quiet drink.

Parties

Parties are even better because you're bound to have a connection, but of course you generally need an invite (but make sure you crash any party you can hear from your flat. By making a noise they're implicitly inviting any neighbours, since they're keeping you awake. And as long as you don't appear mental, most people are pleasantly surprised to meet their neighbours, especially in big cities.)

Always get to parties early. In a packed room you need an excuse to approach a woman, but if there are only four of you, you'd need an excuse not to. The early bird gets the worm, and in this case the early worm gets the bird. If you see a woman you like, do the groundwork early. Get to know her, do your mingling, and then start talking to her a bit later on when the party livens up, and everyone's had a bit more to drink. Then make your approach: whether you're going in for a kiss, suggesting you move on, or just getting her number and arranging to meet another time. If it's the last of these, leave now. Don't ruin it by getting pissed and unsuccessfully trying it on with another woman there.

Weddings and funerals

Weddings are, for obvious reasons, a great place to pull. The drink is free, there are loads of young people around, and there's an air of coupling (the whole reason you're there). Funerals, though, can also be lively events, although this obviously only works if it's a 'happy' funeral involving a relative who died in his 100s surrounded by loving family and a big pile of inheritance-tax exempt cash. The drink is also free and it's a chance to meet plenty of women you haven't seen since you were seven. In Ireland funerals were traditionally the number one matchmaking arena – after all, the family have just lost a member, so it's a good time to start creating new ones. Still, try not to make any jokes about 'stiffs.'

According to a survey conducted by something called the Martini Flirting Society, 27 per cent of British couples met in a pub, a slightly depressing fact for anti-alcohol campaigners.

Non-alcoholic environments

American pulling guides tend to stress the mating opportunities offered by shopping centres, coffee shops and other daytime locations, pointing out that bars and clubs are for losers. I'm sceptical about this, being from the UK where pubs are more acceptable and less like Mo's Bar in *The Simpsons*. While my local drinking establishment has probably produced more ill advised couplings than Woodstock, I've never heard of anyone who got lucky in Tesco. Maybe it's a British thing, but for better or worse, alcohol is king in Britain; it helps us to loosen up after a hard day working the long hours in Europe. The one advantage that shops and other unlikely places do have, however, is that women don't expect to be chatted up and therefore her shield is down; that means there's less pressure on you as well.

Coffee shops do have some potential, in that they are often full of women alone reading their book. If you're into books, and she's reading one you've read (or seen the film of, at least), then it provides a decent icebreaker. The upside is that coffee shops are far less sexually charged, and it's easier to appear like a natural and friendly person; the downside is a lot of women come here to read and be left alone.

If you're interested in picking up foreign women, coffee and teashops, especially in London or in student or tourist towns, are a good place to find your desired market.

Model-turned-photographer Lia Emmerson on supermarket sweet-talking

'While in Sainsbury's, I headed towards the meat counter and found some steak I wanted to buy. I reached out and placed my hand on it, when another hand rested upon mine. A voice then said, 'Well you have the salad, I'll buy the meat and we could make a night of it.' I was so taken aback I went bright red and ridiculously muttered I needed it for a facial. I later left the shop and saw him leaving in a TVR. Oh how I hated myself!'

Gay clubs

There was a time when these were the most popular place to meet women, but gay clubs tend to lose their sense of fun once boozy straight men cotton on to the fact that they're full of women. Which is slightly annoying for them, as women are there to escape beer-stained lechy womanisers; still, they tend to have great atmospheres and the ladies have their guards down. And simply by being there you're showing that you're an outgoing, adventurous man who's not afraid of doing something different.

Martin from London

'I've only been to two gay clubs and I pulled both times (with women, obviously). I'm not normally the best looking in the club, and in those nights I was positively the worst. But after a night of dancing, the women are really in the mood and, hey, I suppose I was the best available thing.'

7

First Contact

The worst thing you can do is get flustered, which is why advice about 'first impressions' is often counter-productive. First impressions don't matter one bit – keep that in mind and you'll never have trouble with the opposite sex. You can always correct initial mistakes and worrying about how you appear to girls will just make you nervous. Psychological tests have shown that last impressions remain in the memory far longer and stronger than first. Which is good news, as these are far less nerve-wrecking, and you're less likely to bugger them up, unless you trip on the carpet on the way out of the pub.

Eye contact

In soppy romance films, the most important story point is the moment when a man and woman spot each other across a crowded room, or on opposite escalators, or whatever corny setting they've contrived. Of course in these movies the self-assured little prick in the lead role, knowing that the woman is going to fancy his arse off, just stares at her until she looks over and realises she's head over heels in love.

The actor probably had to do 27 takes (plus time in make-up) before he had the perfect dashing look, but you'll only have one, so don't beat yourself up about it. Just be assured that if the woman holds your gaze, you have a chance.

It's a fine balancing act. Look away immediately and you look either shifty or like a feeble weed; too long and she'll think you've just done a runner from Broadmoor.

Smile, and the world smiles with you

Humans like to smile; it releases small amounts of the happy hormones called endorphins, and it takes less effort than a frown. Smiling feels good, but it's also contagious, so smiley people tend to be more popular than misery guts. A lot of people have got it into their heads that looking sultry makes them more attractive, but this is a trick that can be pulled off by only a tiny proportion of people; everyone else just looks miserable and angry. *Nuts* gets about a dozen submissions a day from wannabe glamour models, and the biggest mistake a lot of them make is to pull an angry face in the mistaken belief it makes them sexy. It just makes them look like they're hating every minute of being photographed, and would be a pain to work with.

The same thing goes for men; we think that by glaring we look like Steve McQueen in *The Great Escape*; that look is easy to pull off if you're on a motorbike being chased by German prison guards, but at a party it's not so appropriate. So whenever you walk through a doorway, whether it's a party, pub or just a coffee shop, smile.

And various scientific tests have shown that the great majority of smiles (more than 75 per cent) will be met with a smile back.

How to catch her gaze

Ever get the feeling you're being looked at? Humans have a sixth sense that allows them to tell if someone or something is staring at them, even with their back's turned, a theory backed by laboratory experiments. It's an added warning system that helped our ancestors escape the many perils of the jungle, but the bonus is that you can make a woman aware of your presence even if she is stuck in conversation, or walking down the road.

Firstly, if you see a girl in conversation, don't let her out of your sights; no matter how interesting the person she's talking to appears, at some point her gaze will wander and when this happens look her way in a sure, confident manner. Once your eyes meet, smile and let her break the stare. If she smiles back, gets flustered, or looks down before looking away, she probably likes you; if she simply looks away, probably not. But you've done the groundwork for an approach.

Always be warned, though, that a lot of good signals are also just signs of general nerves.

The approach

Whether it's at a party, with someone you might make a connection with or a random girl in a pub, the secret is to be mindless. Think like the confident idiots you remember from school, or in other words, don't think at all. Don't get introspective or thoughtful, as these are great qualities for poets but terrible ones for men of action, and you want to be a man of action. Thinking will only sap your bravery. Read any article about a 'have a go' hero or someone who did something very courageous, and they always say that they weren't thinking when they performed their act of heroism, they just did it on instinct. Had they had time to ponder the consequences, chances are they would have lost their nerve.

That's why the three-second rule, makes perfect sense; by approaching a woman before you have time to chicken out, you increase your chances dramatically.

Don't worry what you're going to say either; even if it goes wrong and the barrel-toned oratory voice you practised goes out of the window, it's better even to blurt out something inane than lose your bottle altogether.

Chances are she'll be just as flustered, and won't begrudge you talking nonsense; you can always rescue the situation by making a joke of your gibberish.

Remember, what counts is your confident manner, not what you say. Once you engage her in conversation, your confidence will grow, your heartbeat will slow down, and your trail of thought will become clearer. What matters most is making the initial contact.

Not everything you say has to be pure wit; if you actually analysed most human chit-chat, you'd find that most people talk useless rubbish most of the time; the very act of communicating is what matters. Chimpanzees, our closest relative, spend 20 per cent of their day picking nits out of each other, a complete overkill on the nit-picking front, but a way of smoothing over social relations. When humans learned to talk we found that this was a much better way of keeping the tribe united, so we stopped wasting all that time playing with our hair, giving us more time for making small talk. But the principle is the same: simply by talking to someone, you're making it clear that you're not a threat but a potential friend, and possibly more than that. And while there is no way everything you say will be interesting, original or funny, don't worry because she'll only remember the very good, or very bad, bits, not the filler somewhere in-between.

And another thing – always approach from the front, so she can see you coming; you never want to tap a woman to get her attention, and if her back is turned to you to start with, you have an extra hill to climb.

Breaching the shield – direct v indirect approaches

Man's biggest problem in the pulling game is overcoming a woman's natural defences. Every woman has a sort of anti-suitor shield that is there to deter timewasters, and this usually comes with an inbuilt weirdo-detector and dickhead-neutralising beam (which admittedly doesn't work with some women). The more a woman is chatted up, the stronger these defences are, to prevent her from getting involved with losers and low-grade males.

Direct approaches have the advantage of being honest – you're upfront and she may feel more comfortable because you're not being sly. If the woman is about the same status as you, in other words you're both average looking, then direct approaches are also best.

Where the indirect approach comes in handy is with girls you'd normally consider out of your league; there's no point telling an absolutely gorgeous girl that she's stunning, because of course she knows this already, and it will only reinforce her belief that you are below her in status, a major deal-breaker. In which case start a casual conversation by asking her opinion on something, such as what there is to do in the area, and present a relaxed, disinterested air, the way you would with any male you started talking to.

It's also the case that women have become more sophisticated about male approaches. Going up to a woman and saying, 'Your dad must be a thief because he stole an angel from heaven,' will instantly set her alarm bells ringing, and she'll clam up. But by making simple statements, engaging in conversation, and paying as much attention to her friends as to her, she may open up enough to give you a chance. And once her shield has allowed you past those defences, 90 per cent of your work is done.

Louise from London
'It's very attractive if someone is attracted to you. I only started to think of my current boyfriend as 'boyfriend material' when he made it clear he fancied me; suddenly I saw him in a different light.'

Openers and ice-breakers

Firstly don't smash some ice on the table and say, 'Now I've broken the ice, we can get down to it.' I've never heard of a chat-up line actually working, except when said with a very big tongue in cheek, but if you do have the gall to pull it off with a smile on your face, go ahead. The problem is that when you directly approach a woman, it is obvious you are there for one thing; she knows it, and we know she knows it, but instead of just being blunt about the whole thing, we have to go through a mating ritual.

In a purely logical universe the mating ritual would go like this:

Man: Would you like to partake in recreational sexual intercourse with me?
Woman: Affirmative/negative.

Chat-up lines work on the principle that you approach a woman directly, making your interests clear, amazing her with a bombardment of bullshit, or that you can look smooth enough to pull it off. While once they have may have worked, we've all become a bit too cynical about the whole thing; just as you might be about a double glazing salesman in a silver suit and a spiv moustache.

And even if she is speaking to the most ugly man in the world, don't say you're rescuing her from him, unless you're 100 per cent sure she doesn't like him. I've read advice where people suggest you pick up the pieces after another man's lame attempt by saying 'that's the worst pick-up I've ever seen,' but don't put down other men unless he's earned the right to have the piss taken by obnoxious or rude behaviour. She may think you're putting on an act, or he might turn out to be her disabled brother, in which case you have a lot of groundwork to make up.

Some good openers:
Do say

- 'Where did you buy that top?' Tell her you admire her outfit. You're not being corny by saying 'You're a pretty thing.' Instead you're complimenting her taste and, therefore, her personality.

- 'Can we share your table?'

- 'So, how was your day?'

- 'Would you like a drink?'

- 'My friend here is new in town. Could you recommend some good bars?'

- Alternatively, say 'Hi' to a girl you don't know and use an eyebrow flash (simultaneously raising both, as you would with someone you are on nodding terms with), causing her to respond in some way, often a 'Hi' back or a 'do I know you?' And even though you can always bail out by pretending to mistake her for a friend, part of her will think she must know you, for long enough at least for you to start a conversation. Remember, like with starting a career, getting your foot in the door is the most important thing.

Don't say
(Unless, of course, you're mindlessly confident, in which case anything you say can work.)

- Any sort of sexual compliment. Wait until you've connected with her before bringing up the subject of sex.

- 'I just have to thank you for brightening up my day.'

- 'Want to see my elephant impression?'

- 'What's your favourite font?'

- If you've bumped into each other; 'Oh, don't worry. You would have stopped me in my tracks even if you weren't blocking my way!'

- But funniest of all is the approach recommended by one contributor to FastSeduction.com, a popular website where users compare their seduction technique, who says, 'A friend of mine simply grunts 'SEX!' at women, that's it. Seems to work about ten per cent of the time.' Which is quite a good success rate, considering.

And remember, maintain eye contact throughout, speak slowly and clearly, and pause before statements. A good pauser will always go far in life.

Traditional chat-up lines

Just for the sake of record, I've included a few of these corkers, only to be said with a mouth full of irony and a belly full of liquid courage:

- 'Do you sleep on your front? Do you mind if I do?'

- 'Is that a mirror in your pocket? Only I can see myself in your pants!'

- 'Did it hurt? When you fell from Heaven?'

- 'If I could rearrange the alphabet I would put 'U' and 'I' together.'

- 'Do you believe in love at first sight or should I walk past you again?'

- 'Get your coat, love, you've pulled.'

- 'How do you like your eggs? Fertilised?'

- 'Are your legs hurting because you have been running through my mind all night?'

- 'If I told you I loved your body would you hold it against me?'

8

Pack Hunting

Humans are pack animals, as anyone who's seen a group of blokes pissing against a wall will realise. Alone, we're puny little things with weak muscles (a chimp is eight times as strong as a man) and no natural weapons, which is why there is such stigma attached to being a loner, or 'Billy No Mates' as they get christened at school.

But we don't just hunt in numbers; like cheetahs we also court in teams (pairs of cheetah brothers will look for females together as 'coalitions', and often share them, which means that at the very least they get to be an uncle). We do something similar with wingmen. (Although after initially making contact, the seduction process itself is a one-on-one affair, unless, of course, you're a professional footballer.)

Good pulling partners

Your chances of getting lucky depend largely on the company you keep, so remember to be careful who you shark with. Some will cramp your style, so never make the mistake of hanging out with someone because he makes you look good. Women judge a man by their friends, and if your mates are all a waste of oxygen, she'll just think you're chief loser; there's also the fact that if she does go off with you, she doesn't want her friends stuck with a bunch of idiots. On the other hand, going to a bar with a real stud will help you meet women, and even if you're feeding off his leftovers, it's better than a date with Mr Doner, purveyor of finest kebab meat.

But while some friends make great team mates in the game of pulling, others, however close, are saboteurs. Either they resent anyone else getting the girl, or they're so crass and inept that they alienate all women and bring you down in the meantime. Pack pulling is about having a partner you can trust and rely on; it's a bit like strike partnerships in football – some great strikers just don't gel together, while others (your Beardsley and Linekers, Sheringham and Shearers) work like a well-oiled machine, complimenting each other and using their strengths for the good of the team.

If you and your friend are not an instinctive natural pairing, make sure you establish some rules first: if both of you abide by them, you'll do just fine.

The wingman rules

Never put each other down

A bit of friendly banter is no bad thing, but put your friend down and not only will his confidence suffer, but any woman with half a brain will think you're a dick as well. Having a mean-spirited attitude to your friend getting lucky will only end up hurting you.

Introduce each other

This is a more grown-up version of 'my mate fancies you,' but it works. If you know your friend has the eye for a certain girl, wait until he goes to the toilet, then approach her and say, 'I know I shouldn't do this, but my friend over there won't stop talking about you.' Rave about how great he is in every way, and don't be scared to make yourself seem idiotic if it helps him. He'll really appreciate it if it works, and will one day do the same for you.

Set each other up for jokes

Most men like to be the centre of female attention and it can be hard when the other guy gets the laughs, but if a couple of women are laughing, it means they're comfortable, and if they're comfortable, you're both in with a chance. You shouldn't be jealous of her laughing at him any more than if you took her to see a stand-up comedian, which would have cost you money.

Casually mention good things about him

Good things you've done – whether you ran the marathon, performed an emergency appendectomy once on the bus, or help out at the homeless shelter once in a while – always sounds three times as impressive if they come from someone else who doesn't have an agenda. But don't make it look like a pre-rehearsed routine, and don't lie, because women have far better bullshit detectors than we do. And if you claim your Primark-clad friend owns a Hedge Fund firm, hers will go off like a prison alarm when a visitor turns up carrying a very large cake with a metal-looking thing sticking out.

Never go for the same girl

This is absolutely crucial, as a double whammy will scare her off, have you working against each other, and ultimately end with two men going home alone and with one less friend.

Give your friend a chance with a girl if he spoke to her first

The law of 'bagsy' doesn't really have much legal weight after the age of nine, but there is an unspoken rule that the man who makes the approach is free to try his luck without anyone cramping his style. Don't turn up a minute later and try starting a conversation over him; give your friend a chance and after half an hour or so; if it becomes apparent that she wouldn't sleep with him even if it were the only way of stopping some wrathful god from making the crops fail, then you can step in, in a gentlemanly way.

Always take one for the team

There may come a time when your friend is with a lady and looks like she might let him dock in her port, but only if you get comfortable with her friend, the unfortunate looking one you were both laughing at back when the evening was innocent. Well, sometimes a man's gotta do... something unsavoury, when his friend is in need.

The seduction saboteur

Beauties often hit the town in pairs, but just as often an attractive woman will go out with a less attractive friend. They may be intellectual and financial equals, but unfortunately they cannot ever forget about the cruel inequality of the cards they were dealt in life, because men swarm around the pretty girl and give her their most charming spiel, but sneer when the other one tries to join the conversation, or simply ignore her. For this reason the seduction saboteur has learned to try to fight off any male approach.

Who can blame her? Men can't really see her point of view because we do the approaching, but imagine being

Colin Farrell's best mate and trying to go to the pub with him, being ignored all night as women tried to write their name in lipstick on his shirt, strangling him with their knickers, and getting him to autograph their boobs.

Women being a lot nicer than men, they also get angry at how potential suitors are so two-faced in the way they treat their less good-looking friends, so it's vital you don't alienate her snappy sidekick.

Instead, try to befriend her. Approach her first, then keep her in the conversation, smile at her, and be as friendly and polite as you possibly can, but don't flirt; if you do that the good-looking one will think, 'Ah bless, Imelda's got a fella.' If her friend is laughing at all your jokes the looker will notice, and start to make some ticks next to your name. Don't just ignore the other girl when she joins the conversation: divide your attention between them until the right times comes to make a pass at the chosen girl.

The same goes for her male friends. If you are pleasant to them and win them over, they're far less likely to sabotage you, and unless they are the girls' boyfriends (and that will soon be obvious) men out with female friends aren't going to stop them pulling as long as the new man doesn't try to threaten them or usurp their status. It would make them look stupid, after all.

Going solo

Alternatively you might be on a one-man mission, in which case the most important disadvantage you have to counter is the suspicion that you're weird. You can neutralise this fear if:

- You're in a strange town on business, in which case it's natural you'll want to hit the bars, and are looking for natives to show this mysterious, interesting gentlemen around.

- In a crowded club late at night. Friends lose each other all the time, so you can always pretend this has happened.

- You're killing time before meeting friends (this helps because she'll be reassured you're not sticking around forever).

- If you can assure her with a convincing explanation, you might prefer to do your work away from prying eyes and the pressure of friends. In other words, if she has a 'nice personality'.

9

Boy Band Theory –
How To Specialise

What do you see when you look in the mirror? What nicknames do your friends give you? How will women describe you when they have to ask someone for your name? The tall bloke? The bald fella? The oddball who doesn't stop talking about train gauges? Within minutes you will have given a woman a fair idea of what sort of man you are; it's difficult to completely fake it, but you can put a spin on your identity and present a more flattering picture of yourself.

Have a USP

There's generally no excuse for using terms from the world of corporate bullshit, but 'unique selling point' is a good one nonetheless. Many women will decide to sleep with a man simply because he knows a lot about shoes, or can dance well, or is knowledgeable about the obscure US state she's from. Specialisation is the key to human survival, and the best way of maximising your success in the workplace, so there's no surprise that it's also the key to many a woman's chastity belt.

Women might go for certain things – confidence, charm, wit, nice eyes, musical abilities and generosity – but before they find Mr Right, they're prepared to kiss a lot of frogs just because they have one of these things in abundance. If you are skilled in one area, specialise in it. If wit is not your thing, don't try to fake it; likewise if you're not an easy-going party animal but you do have self-belief, maximise this element of your personality and don't pretend to be something you're not by dressing up like Fat Boy Slim in a Hawaiian shirt.

Kate from Gloucester says:
'Women are impressed by knowledge, even trivia, as long as you don't try to be a know all. We like to know there's something going on in a man's brain. And there are so many thick men about, it makes a change.'

Mr Mystery

Women absolutely love a man of mystery, which is why it's vital to never impart too much information about yourself. If you seem mysterious, they'll ask themselves key questions like:

- What does he do for a living?

- What does his flat look like?

- How many women has he been out with?

- How does he relax?

And, given that many women are nurtured on a diet of corny romance in the books they read and films they watch, maybe they'll come to the logical conclusion that you have a penthouse flat in Mayfair, drive a Mercedes, and play polo with aristocrats on the weekend when you're not parachuting into Afghanistan to fight the Taliban with the help of the local warlord. In other words, some sort of James Bond character.

There's no need to lie about yourself, but don't offer up information that reflects badly on you, even if it gets a cheap laugh. If you've been out of a relationship for ages or your last six girlfriends all dumped you after a month, keep this to yourself and don't use it as the basis of a joke. If you do she'll laugh, but she won't go near you if romance is what you're offering.

And also another reason for not talking about yourself too much is that women love to talk about themselves; always turn the conversation back to her, and this applies even if she's fascinated by you or your job or where you come from. In fact, especially so.

A breath of fresh air

Newcomers in any small town have a huge advantage with the local ladies, simply because women easily get bored with men who all act alike. You'll often see this with any group of blokes, especially younger ones, whether they work together, all follow the same type of music, or even just hang out in the same bar or club. Men are pack animals, and basically cowards, which is why we all follow the leader; put some men in a room together and they'll all start imitating the speech, mannerisms and even social attitudes of the dominant male. I've even known of offices all developing a single accent, mimicking the laugh and vowel sounds of the dominant male.

Women find this very boring, so just being a bit different makes you an instant catch. You'll appear like an individual with his own ideas, even if back in your hometown you are just another drone. This is why lads' weekends away always produce a much higher success rate than those spent in your local – the women there have heard it all before.

This also applies to your approach; if you're in a club

or bar and you notice that the men all address women in the same way, such as offering them a drink, asking their names or dancing the same, do something completely different; even if it's in itself a rubbish approach, you'll score points just for being a novelty.

A man of the world

There's something attractive about a man who's lived life, travelled to exotic places and had interesting jobs. Obviously this is a hard act if you're 18, but at the very least show some plans to travel, do something different, see the world. There's nothing worse than a bloke who has no ambitions further than his local.

Knowledge is a great thing, so try to have a basic understanding of the following areas:

- How things work. Cars, bicycles, or DIY; enough so that you might be useful if something broke down. Women love a handyman; so casually mention that you refurbished your entire flat, playing down the fact that most of it was done by a Polish builder.

- Food and drink. You don't necessarily have to be a wine-spitting connoisseur, but do have some idea about good food and booze –James Bond would not have been quite the sex bomb had his signature drink been

'lager top' rather than vodka Martini.
Knowing how to cook, even a tiny bit,
is also a great quality, especially if your
friend mentions it to her.

- Culture. Do you know your music and film?
Few young men read novels, but most
women do. Do you know interesting facts
about film? The story behind certain love
songs? This kind of info sprinkled into
conversation makes you sound far more
interesting. But no science fiction,
fantasy or *Dungeons and Dragons* stuff –
this is negative knowledge that will impress
geeks but repulse women.

- What to do. Do you know what's going
on, what's playing around town? Cultural
events like plays, live performances and
anything to do with art exhibitions are always
more popular with women than men.

- People. Does your cousin work in a restaurant?
Give him a call. Girls love a man who can
get a good table. Likewise your old school
friend who's in charge of guest lists at a club.
Ring him up, even if you secretly hate him.
Being connected is a very attractive quality;
think back to the great rock bands of the
1970s – it was the roadies who saw more
action than the actual band members.

Images to avoid

- Lazy – Homer Simpson is an icon to men everywhere, but no sex symbol.

- Unadventurous – women often drag their boyfriends into boring exhibitions or unsavoury back street clubs where everyone looks like they want to kill someone, and then saying, 'Don't be so boring,' when he asks if they can leave. So at least pretend you're up for anything.

- Unambitious – ambition is attractive. Banks will lend students a great deal of money because they have the potential to become rich in later life; for the same reason women will fall for you if you have the air of someone going somewhere.

- Mean – girls hate a tight-arse. Biologists think that generosity evolved because women went for the most generous males; perhaps they were most likely to win friends or feed her family as well as his. So don't skimp on drinks, tip waiters generously, and even if you know he's going to spend it on White Lightning, give money to any pathetic looking beggars.

Your persona – Boy Band Theory

Have you ever noticed that in manufactured boy bands each of the little turds has their own 'personality', and that everything from their clothes and haircut to the lines they're fed by sinister managers are geared up towards drumming into everyone's heads that these men each has a magic quality? That's so their girl followers can hone in on the one that possesses their particular favoured male strength.

There are basically four or five different types of men who do well with women.

1. The Tough Guy. Usually the biggest one in the band, who's made to have a line shaved into his hair and given 'street' clothes to emphasise just how damn hard he is, even if he did go to stage school.

2. The Feminine One. The girly-looking, soft-faced, non-threatening sensitive type, who inevitably 'bravely' comes out of the closet to a tabloid that otherwise would have outed him, leaving millions of girls heartbroken.

3. The Funny Boy. Usually not actually funny, but more 'wacky' than the others and likely to do crazeee things on stage and in interviews; probably addicted to painkillers.

4.   The Suave Chap. Dressed to kill and
always wearing a £200 pair of jeans, he
can't walk past a mirror without spending
20 minutes doing his hair.

5.   The Entertainer. In other words, the
show-off: basically the only one who
can sing as well as dance, and act. At least
in panto. He's attractive because he has
these 'gifts' he can give women.

6.   The Clever Clogs. The manager who is
making a fat pile of cash out of these chumps.

Now you don't have to be in a boy band to be one of
these types; they're everywhere, and if one of them
even vaguely fits you, play up to it. Develop that part
of you, emphasising it in the way you act, and gaining
a reputation as either comedian, entertainer, tough guy
and so on. This is far better than trying to have a bit of
everything and ending up failing miserably when you
lose a fight or a joke falls flat.

To thine ownself be true

Trying to be something you're not is always a waste
of time, but especially so when it comes to girls. If
you can't dance and hate loud music, then clubs aren't
going to be happy hunting ground for you, unless you
bump into the one girl who also hates it; likewise if
your idea of literature is the paperback spin-off of

Spiderman (with pictures), then mincing around Costa Coffee asking girls what they're reading is not going to produce much of a result, especially if you then start explaining why you loved Andy McNab's latest work. Big, raucous suburban drinking factories with bouncers out front are great for girls, but if you're intimidated by the louts or put off by the directness of the women, why bother? There's something for everyone in the market.

Don't fake it

Humour is not the be all and end all, so don't fake it. There's no one more painful than the man who repeats last night's comedy word for word but with all the wit removed, or the 'joke assassin' who causes the room to go dead with a witless aside to a humorous conversation. David Brent is such a successful character because he's so typical of naturally unfunny men who are desperate to get a laugh. Better to let other people do the clowning than be a failed funny man.

Don't worry about it. Most of Hollywood's A-List could never pull off a comic role, and they do all right on the female front.

What's her type?

Successful seducers soon become very skilled at working out what types a woman goes for. Sure you can often tell by her clothes, so if she's wearing beads and a

Greenpeace badge, offering her a ride in your Hummer won't go down a (global warming related) storm. But there are more subtle pointers, most of which you can gauge from her in casual conversation:

- What's her ideal quality in a man?

- Is she looking for Mr Right or just a bit of fun?

- Does she want a dominant man, an equal, or someone to control?

- Does she want to be protected? Spoiled?

- What were her previous boyfriends like? Where did they go wrong?

- How do you rate her and how high are her standards? Does she only go out with men she considers good-looking?

You can get an idea of the answers by asking certain questions, such as which celebrities she fancies.

Bad boys and good boys

Did you know that tests show women are attracted to different men at different times of the menstrual cycle? In 1999 St. Andrews University asked groups of women in

Scotland and Japan to look at pictures of two sets of chaps during their most and least fertile times of the month. During the most productive period they went for men with strong cheekbones, deep-set eyes and prominent jaw lines; on other days they fancied chaps with soft skin, big eyes and gentle, thin noses. Now, you're inclined to wonder, why are women so complicated when we're so simple? There are reasons for this, and it's vital in understanding what attracts women.

The reason fertile women show a preference for masculine-looking men like George Clooney, Ross Kemp and Daniel Craig is because they showed manly traits, the same qualities that a woman would want her son to carry. But when less fertile, women fancied soft-faced men like David Beckham and Leonardo Di Caprio because they associated their boyish (even girly) looks with good child-rearing qualities. The obvious conclusion is that women want the children of big butch blokes, but want the nice guys because they'll be good providers and will pay the bills on time. Of course none of these things count consciously when you're on a dance floor, but they still matter. 'He's so cute,' translates as: 'He looks like he'd stick by me when all the water runs out and the lions start trying to eat us.' Whether girly-faced men are better fathers we can't say, but they are certainly less likely to be wandering alpha males who will leave her up the duff.

So two different types: strong, and sensitive. They want to marry Leonardo Di Caprio but have George Clooney's kids. Unfortunately for them, you might be the best available alternative.

Do a Groundhog Day

In the comedy *Groundhog Day*, Bill Murray's character immediately uses his weird curse to try to chat up women, as most of us probably would. He asks a lady what school she went to and what her teachers were called, and the following day, when life repeats itself exactly, he uses his knowledge as a conversational opener to pull her. But this can be done in real life if you're smart enough. Learn to be a bit like Sherlock Holmes and try to assess her. For example:

- What types of music does she seem to be enjoying?

- Does she have any jewellery, and what type? Does she wear one of those coloured silicone wristbands? Depending on the colour she could be giving her support to cancer victims, the starving millions, or an Xbox 360 launch event.

- Is she tanned?

- Is she dressing to highlight a particular part of her body (and not just the obvious)? If so, compliment her on it.

- What colours does she like to wear? They can be significant. Women who wear red may like to stand out and want to look sexy. Blue emits calm, while green suggests the natural look.

The pecking order and giant killing

As its name suggests, the term 'pecking order' originates from the study of chickens, and the hierarchy in which the strongest cocks and hens get their claws on the pick of the grub before leaving all the sweepings to the weaker ones. The same principles works in school discos, although some men have a habit of pulling women who seem to be out of their league –the 'giant-killers' of the seduction world.

Schoolboys used to call the system of ranking a woman out of ten 'the Helen scale', named after the Ancient Greek princess who was so stunning that a fight between two men over her led to the 'launching of 1,000 ships' and a ten-year war that ended with the destruction of the city of Troy (now that's got to turn a girl's head). Yet why do we see so many eights or nines going out with men who'd be a four out of ten at best?

A lot of time they're simply the only men who will ask the girls out. It's true that fantastically good-looking women often get left alone in clubs and pubs, as men assume that they're going to be bitchy, arrogant, and betrothed to a man on the *The Sunday Times* 'Rich List'. It's the just-above-average women who get asked out first.

So don't be scared to approach a real stunner; she may not even know it. Bear in mind that many stunning women were often ugly or spotty teens, or were bullied at school, so there is generally not a correlation between ego and looks.

Lia Emmerson on chatting up models

'I met this guy in a bar and we started talking. He wasn't much of a looker and was too old for my liking, but he was confident in the way he spoke to me, giving me his full attention, talking about his career, achievements and in depth about where he wanted to go in life. I love a man who has set goals in life; whether he is good looking or not, it's a real turn on. If a guy's got the balls to come up to me without his mates and talk to me about his life, ambitions and achievements, then I admire that, and I would prefer an unattractive guy with confidence than a wallflower with good looks.'

Start from the top up

Good-looking women will never go with a man they've seen with a woman of lower status – you're beneath them from that point on. In any meat market it's always best to start from the top; they won't be so insulted if you've just been chatting up a professional model, but they won't take one of Quasimoda's cast-offs. You don't want to get the nickname Iron Mike Dyson because you're famous for picking up all the sweepings from the dance floor, or as Lia Emmerson says, 'In my mind it means that he hasn't got a lot of confidence to ask out really attractive women, it makes me think that this guy just wants to end up in bed!'

And as for the girls in the lower leagues they won't care either; sadly for them, they know they're not going to be able to compete with the Heidi Klums of this world, so it carries few risks.

Pickiness – good or bad?

The coupling game is a bit like the free market – there's something for everyone and, whatever tastes you have, there will be a product or person somewhere to satisfy it. So be as fussy or welcoming as you want with the ladies, but watch out for getting a reputation as a tubby-chaser on the one hand, or making it impossible for yourself on the other. Men with ridiculously high standards often have some mental block where they don't actually want to pull because they're scared, and the longer this goes on, the more scared they get.

10

Mistakes We Make

There are several different ways to charm a woman and we could argue 'til the cows come home about which is the best, and no doubt you'll disagree with some. But there are certain methods guaranteed to screw your chances up.

Chickening out

The most obvious. You see a woman, make eye contact, steady your nerves to approach her, then just as you're about to make her acquaintance, you bottle it, and walk past, pretending to take an interest in the fruit machine. She knows what your plan was. Furthermore, she knows that you know that she knows. This usually comes about because you're thinking about what you're doing, and all of a sudden a little panicky voice says, 'What are you going to say to her?'

This can only be avoided with practice, and by firstly approaching women in less stressful situations, such as a less busy bar and when neither you or she is in a big group. Tell yourself that if it all goes wrong then that is a good thing, a result. Every approach you make is a success in itself.

Desperation

There was once a bizarre episode of *Neighbours* when a rock star turned up in town. I wasn't sure if it was a real Aussie rock star; the slightly surreal nature of the incident suggested he was. Either way, he said one thing that rung true: women can smell desperation. Maybe in years to come scientists will prove that men start to smell different if they haven't had sex for ages. Either way women can always tell from these signs:

- Making a move too early, whether it's laying it on thick, moving too close too soon, or trying to kiss her when she's not warmed up.

- Pushing for a date as soon as possible. Always suggest it a few days in advance.

- Saying 'How about Thursday?' when she says she can't do Wednesday. Instead, let her offer an alternative date.

- Any sort of pleading or panicking. If she wants to go off and speak to her friends, let her. If you act cool about it, she may come back.

Apologising

Never say sorry for approaching a woman, unless you're Hugh Grant, in which case it may just work. You're not inconveniencing her by talking, so why should you apologise? People who say 'sorry' all the time are annoying. But be polite; by all means say, 'You don't mind if I join you,' but don't say, 'Sorry for joining you.'

Acting too coarse

You should always treat a woman with respect, even if she is turning the air blue outside a club in Faliraki.

Acting like a gentleman has become so rare that, like with any skill in any market, its value has gone up.

Good manners go a long way, because they make other people feel good and respected, and so work especially when you're talking to women. A lot of men forget that by treating someone with respect and politeness, you make it about 1000 times easier to get them to do what you want. And acting like a gentleman is very easy, there being only a handful of things to remember.

- Open doors for women.

- Offer to help with heavy items. Men have 50 per cent greater upper body strength, so we may as well use it.

- Stand up when you're introduced to a woman.

- Shake her hand, and don't just mumble 'Aright?' Take every opportunity to get tactile with a woman, but obviously don't grab her arse.

- Offer to buy her a drink, especially if she isn't your chosen target. Some people consider this patronising, but men still earn far more than women, and most of the time this isn't deserved. The unequal distribution of drink-buying is nature's way of equalising this injustice. But don't buy her more than one (see 'Submission' below).

- If it's cold, lend her your coat, especially if it means you have to see her another time to retrieve it.

- Don't swear. Men who mainly socialise with other men tend to swear a lot, forgetting that a lot of women aren't impressed and associate it with having a small vocabulary.

All of these tips will impress about 90 per cent of women. Of course if she is vomiting outside a club while shouting, 'Oi, oi, saveloy!', she'll probably think there's something wrong with you, and likewise if she's a serious feminist (and not the sort of 'feminist' who thinks flashing her knickers and downing eight Bacardi Breezers is liberated) she may feel affronted. But they are very much in the minority.

On that note don't for a minute confuse chivalry with sexism. Sexism is based on the idea that women are mentally inferior, while chivalry is based on the fact that men are physically stronger and use that strength not to rule but to help. Chivalry might be politically incorrect, but PC men don't tend to do very well in this game.

If you don't even know what chivalry is, rent out old films starring the likes of Carey Grant, Spencer Tracey and James Stewart. These men had old school manners down to a tee, and there isn't a woman outside of the golf circuit who wouldn't snap them up.

Submission

But don't confuse being a gent with being submissive. Treat her with respect but demand respect in return, and don't approach her like a medieval peasant would his queen. Whatever their financial status or looks, no one, male or female, has the right to talk down to anyone because of their genetic luck, and if you let her treat you like an idiot, she will almost certainly never sleep with you. Don't just accept this behaviour because she's gracing you with her company and you hope it will lead to something more, because it won't. Look out for these warning signs:

- Not buying any drinks. If you've bought her a glass already, next time round she should offer to buy one; if she doesn't, simply say you have to go. Even better, tell her that it's her round. I've made the mistake of paying for everything before and it's led to nothing but a slightly threatening letter from the bank.

- Turning away from you. If she only talks to you when she wants something, or her favoured company goes to the loo, and then sits with her back to you the rest of the time, ignore her. Talk to everyone else instead until she's worked out you're not an idiot.

- Flirting with other men. If she does this, ignore her and, if she doesn't take the hint, walk away.

Arrogance

Many men try to over-do the confidence thing and end up appearing arrogant. It's a hard call because while confidence is so desired, arrogance is hated. Arrogance means thinking you're better than other people, but it suggests deep insecurities, while confidence tends to be quieter but more solid. Try to avoid any of these mistakes:

- Only talking to the good-looking women. Unless she's a complete bitch and cares only about herself, she's not going to be happy with a man who ignores her friend, especially a friend with low self-esteem.

- Bragging. Never boast about something you've done; if you've just climbed Everest or saved someone's life with only a biro and a Swiss army knife while dressed in your best Armani suit, don't mention it, because the chances are someone else will bring it up (hopefully your wingman). And when they do, she's going to be far more impressed, because not only is modesty an added bonus, but it also suggests you've done even more amazing things. Even if you're alone and there's nobody there to act as your PR man, fight the temptation to brag – women can detect inner confidence anyway, so there's no point.

- Showing off. Don't be loud and over the top, so that people four tables away can hear you shout about how much money you made today. Especially don't act like this if you wear a suit to work: you'll look like a city prick.

- Suggesting, in any way, that you assume you've pulled her. Even if all the signs point that way, no woman wants to be taken for granted, so always give the impression she's a challenge. In many cases a woman does want to sleep with you, even right away, but she needs to reassure herself that she's not easy.

- And don't put anyone down, especially men she's talking to. Women might love a bastard, but they certainly don't like a weasel.

Getting drunk

We've all been there. Alcohol might lubricate a lot of social settings, but it sure ruins a lot of dating and mating opportunities; Spanish beach resorts only work despite having overwhelmingly male populations because the majority of the men are too plastered to say anything but their next drink order.

For most of us there is an optimum zone where we're relaxed but coherent, generally somewhere between one and four pints. If you find yourself slipping out of this, ask for a pint of water or some bar snacks. If you're just out to get a number, get it and make your excuses before you ruin it, then join your mates for a great booze-up.

Unrequited love

Like England winning the World Cup, it's never going to happen simply because you want it too much, and if you desire something that badly, your nerves and obvious desperation keep it away from your grasp. Becoming obsessed with a girl who isn't responding to your advances makes it infinitely more difficult to win her over.

Never, ever stick around for unrequited love, because the more she sees you, the less your chance of getting anywhere. If you love a girl and you think that by being on her case you can change her mind, you're wasting your time, because she will never, ever have sex with you. Get out of there and think like the single man that you are.

Female challenges

Just as a potential employer will sometimes give you sneaky questions to test your resolve, women will often lay verbal traps into which fall the chumps and desperados.

The drink challenge
If she asks you to buy her a drink, don't say 'no'

with a grumpy look on your face, but suggest that by buying her a drink, you'd be conforming to a sexist stereotypical gender role that is against your principles, or some other bollocks, but always with a smile on your face. A woman who asks you to buy her a drink takes you for a sucker.

The sex challenge

Many women will say something very coarse, such as a boast about sexual prowess or some other comment designed to make you embarrassed, to test your reactions; and in this challenge there are two options of failure. Either going red and clamming up, or getting excited and offering to take her up on the offer in the toilets in five minutes; instead just congratulate her and take it in your stride, as if that sort of sexual depravity is old news to you.

The ugly friend challenge

'So why don't you hook up with my mate?' she'll ask, to see if you're more suited to her lower status friend with the wonky eyes. Whatever you do, don't be honest; she's looking for an excuse to filter you out, and bad-mouthing her unfortunate-looking pal will guarantee your exit. Instead tell her the friend is ideal for a mate of yours, and if you get her number, between you you'll be able to arrange it.

The fight challenge

Sometimes a woman will go even further by pitting

you in an argument, or even a fight, with another male to see how much of a 'real man' you are. If this ever happens, tell the man that she's all his or, even better, jokingly offer to pay him to take her off your hands; she'll either see sense, apologise and be all over you, or you're better off without her anyway.

The Friend Zone aka nice guy syndrome

And now the biggest failure of all, and one of the easiest to get sucked into; just as some women are attractive without appearing sexual, a lot of us give off this 'safe' air to ladies we know, so even if we're technically good-looking they won't find us sexy. Our biggest fault is that we're scared of showing our interest in sex, and before long our new female friend is complimenting us about how great we are to talk to, 'like a brother' almost, and the underlying message is this: you don't have a penis.

Why women love bastards

So the girl of your dreams has run off with the same bloke who used to steal your dinner money or happy-slap you? You're not the first man to suffer this fate, and you won't be the last. Even Ireland's most famous poet, William B. Yeats, once wrote in a poem called 'A Prayer For My Daughter' that 'It's certain that fine women eat. A crazy salad with their meat.' Yeats was well-educated, clever, good company and an all round nice guy with a decent income, but the girl of his dreams, Maud Gonne, spurned him for an IRA gunman who was an utter moron. Yeats was gutted, although he probably put it more poetically. And years later his confidence must have dipped to a new low when he made a pass at Gonne's daughter and she too knocked him back. In general, having a knowledge of poetry will do you no harm whatsoever ever in the women stakes, it's just that Miss Gonne was less susceptible to this mode of seduction than to a man with a great big gun.

The truth is that women don't just love bastards. They also love knob ends, tossers, pricks and all the other categories that make up the bad male of the species. These can all be categorised into three or four types, but they all have one thing in common – confidence. What's more confusing is that if you ask a woman why her friend has rejected you for a man who cheated on her with her mum and then talked her into lending him £1000, she'll act amazed and say, 'I don't know what she sees in him.' Then you hear the next week that she has shacked up with the same rogue.

It's difficult to know what women look for in men because they lie, to themselves as well as us. Women know that they should go for caring, tolerant, and sensitive men, but deep down they're attracted to selfish, aggressive, ultra-confident alpha males. Men with caveman-like attitudes to the housework, total disregard for other people, and often more than a passing interest in violence.

Of course Genghis Khan got the girls, and so do most dictators, gang bosses and even terrorists, but it's not just the power that women like; I've met many a woman who swoon at gun-obsessed rappers but none who fantasises about the prime minister. Every rough pub in every city in Britain has the bloke with about seven children scattered about the place, and none of these local ladykillers has attained a place on the IRA's security council or as a Mafia capo, so it can't be the wealth or fame or power that attracts.

It seems strange that women are attracted to violent men, especially when this violence almost always continues inside the house. Men who hit other men are more likely to hit women as well, even if they do love their mums. But we have to remember that until roughly 5,000 years ago, all humans lived in hunter-gatherer societies, where every day was like a bad night in Glasgow city centre; studies of modern hunter-gatherer groups such as the Inuit and less well-known Yanomamo and !Kung (yes, they do have an exclamation mark in their name) show a murder rate up to 80 times higher than in the worst modern cities, and in one Amazonian tribe 60 per cent of men died by murder. So without courts, police and priests to keep order and scare the hell out of us, life gets pretty frightening, and that world was the norm for all of us until very recently: imagine living in a world where the majority of your friends were murdered? You'd be quite happy if your sister married a skinhead. We might all be happy Labradors on the outside, but deep down there's a wolf inside.

Of course this isn't the only reason why you see nutters with girls queuing up for their attention. Some of these men might be charming, or witty, or have some other sort of hold over women. It could be women's upbringing, and the men they knew as kids, especially their fathers. A less scientific explanation is that the women who go for bastards are just idiots.

Or look at some of the cheating bastards. Take, for instance, Grant Mitchell, a violent and cheating bastard. He slept with his wife's mum, for God's sake, yet just because he has a good stare and says, 'Sorry babe,' the women fall at his feet.

And not only do some women stick by boyfriends who cheat on them time after time, some actively seek out men whose fidelity records would horrify us were the tables turned. Even worse are the hopeless bastards, the men who sponge off women and say, 'I need to get my shit together,' but never do.

Aside from the fact that these sorts of men are often charming and very confident in the first place to get all these women, there is biology at work. In all mammals, a small number of males monopolise all the females, and on student campuses, beach resorts and anywhere else where sex is free and easy, a small number of men always have the great majority of sex. Even in sexually liberated cults, the cult leader tends to get most of the nookie while the male followers tend to just get to do the suicide bit.

Why 'nice guys' finish last

There's no need to turn into any of these types, but we can learn from their star qualities. Violent bastards give the appearance of protection; if a woman feels you can look after her, she will definitely be more inclined to look at your bedroom. Likewise, women love nothing more than a man who could spill his seed everywhere if he wished; his previous conquests act as referees on his pulling CV, after all. As for the hopeless bastard, this is a bit of a niche market, but whenever a woman shows a yearning to look after you – by cooking, for instance – always be appreciative.

But most of all – and this you'll notice any time you see one of these types in action – bastards are not scared of showing their sexuality. The typical 'nice guy', 'safe man' or 'frustrated friend' is frightened of revealing any sexual desire, because he thinks in order to be nice to her, he has to cover it up. In a way we all associate sexuality with being bad, and that's why bad guys get the girl.

Nice guys think that, in order for a woman to like him, he has to turn off his sex buttons and become less of a threat to her. She does end up liking him, but she'll never sleep with him.

Women who love real bastards

There is also that extremely strange sub-culture of women who write to serial killers. Almost all mass murderers have their groupies, but in this case it is more the lure of fame that attracts the ladies. You might say that women want to be treated mean or taken roughly, but no one actually wants to be strangled and chopped up into tiny bits. I think it's safe to say that if a woman's previous boyfriend had the nickname 'Strangler', she's best avoided.

Escape from the Friend Zone

Once a woman categorises you as a friend figure, it's hard to get out of the pigeonhole, so prevention is better than cure. There is no mystery as to why women designate men as friends rather than lovers – you'll end up in the friend zone if she likes you but you don't impress her as mating material. It's not like she sizes you up and thinks, 'He's an amazing catch, but I could really do with a male friend right now.'

Make it clear that you like sex from early in the conversation; perhaps not necessarily with her, but with women generally (and without saying 'I love birds, me', as subtlety is the key). Gauge the situation, but talk about sex, describe the sexual encounters of friends (preferably amusing ones), and in the process put the image of you having sex in her head. Make a subtle sexual innuendo, and see how she takes it; don't talk like a *Carry On* character; make it clear that you like it, but don't call sex 'it'. And cultivate a cheeky smile, preferably with a bit of lip-biting – a sexual smile, in other words.

Don't ask her for sisterly advice, such as on the subject of how to succeed with women. By doing this you're giving the impression that you want her as a confidante, a sex-free female friend, and soon she'll have you as her shoulder to cry on (but nothing more) when her rat-faced boyfriend cheats on her yet again.

If she begins to talk about her ex-boyfriend who broke her heart and who she obviously still fancies, immediately change the subject; even if she seems annoyed that you won't be there for her to talk to, it's for the best.

If you've seen someone a couple of times, and realise that what you see as a date is actually just two friends going for a coffee, don't pressure her, and don't go for death or glory by asking her out. Just keep her at arm's length and try playing the field a bit, making you appear more of a catch by being unattainable.

Seeing you with other women will make her see what she was missing in the first place, and she may start to think of you in a different light altogether. On the other hand she might not, but if that's the case then you were wasting your time to start with.

But don't be upset if your new female best friend wants to set you up with a friend; that's not a failure, that's a result, because with her endorsement your chances with this other girl have gone up massively. Of course, her friend may just have a 'nice personality', which will prove a blow to your confidence no end. The best way to handle this is to do the 'let's be friends' routine with the plain girl, but do your utmost to make sure she's not hurt. This way you can use the endorsement the other way round; the plain girl may just subtly push her attractive friend your way, saying 'You know you two would be good together', taking you out of the friend zone altogether. Complicated stuff? Most evolutionists believe the human brain grew so clever not to outfox other animals, but each other; it's why we're so devious by nature.

Be wary of women who collect male friends; some do so for the ego boost of having men slobbering over them, others just like male company (nothing wrong with that, after all). They may keep the potential of sex dangling like a carrot in front of the donkey; if this happens, tell her straight up you're not interested in being her castrated male.

11

How to Pull Her In

Men and women speak the same language, but understand the words differently. It's a bit like a conversation between an American and a Brit; we hear the words they're speaking, but every phrase has a different shade to it. During the Korean War a British officer told his American comrade over the radio that things were 'sticky'. Thinking that this meant the Brits we're doing OK, the Yanks left them to it; when actually 'sticky' was a typically understated British way of saying 'we're getting slaughtered.'

Women are subtle, and talk in hints and code; men are far more literal in the way they communicate. That's why we never pick up on hints, and are terrible at giving the right presents.

Listen

There are other differences in the way we communicate. When a man complains about a problem, he's generally looking for solutions, whether it's being told how to fix a car or being given the number of a good builder. When a woman talks about a problem, she is more likely just getting it off her chest; men's suggested remedies just seem mechanical and lacking in empathy. And because a woman will listen to you, she will expect the same in return; as many men don't listen to anyone but themselves, a bloke who will take it all in, without judgement or mockery, is a rare commodity.

Echo

And it's not enough to listen; anyone can stare at someone with a glazed over look and pretend to be interested. You have to take in what she says, and repeat it back in garbled form, so if she says, 'My friend Suzie really likes guys with long hair – urggh!', begin your reply, 'So this Suzie likes long haired types?', then offer an intelligent comment and something that suggests you have the same world view. It's simple and obvious, but this way you're connecting, a process that will give her warm, cuddly thoughts when she thinks of you, and make her want you to stay.

Ask questions

Everyone likes to talk about themselves; some people pay psychiatrists a fortune just so they can natter about their own dreams purely because no one else is bothered to listen, so good questioners are worth their weight in gold. Ask her about her job, her friends, her ambitions and dreams, where she likes to go on holiday and what she goes for in a man. If you can get a woman talking about herself for ten, twenty or thirty minutes, she will likely give you her number and look forward to meeting you again, just so she can finish telling you about every single person in her family, circle of old school friends, colleagues and former pets.

Ask open questions, those that begin with how or why. Closed questions are those that can be answered 'yes' or 'no', and these lead to verbal cul-de-sacs if she's not hot on you to start with, because by doing so you're not offering her a chance to expand the conversation.

And don't talk about yourself; if she's interested, she'll ask questions, but let her tell you her life story first.

Praise her

Make her feel good about herself; make it clear you find her good company and you're having a great time with her. She'll feel happy and associate that feeling with you. If she tells you her job, say you bet she's great at it, especially if it involves social skills.

Be positive

Some people have a way with sarcastic comedy, but if you're not Ricky Gervais, try to avoid appearing negative. It's easy to say something nasty, but it can backfire on you. If the music being played is awful or the bar's decor is ridiculous, be gentle with the humour, and don't just moan; you'll sound as much fun as an old person at a bus stop complaining that the bus is late again.

Think ahead

Always have a couple of questions ready at the back of your mind; women can do this sort of mental preparation while listening because their brains are much better at multitasking, but we have to work at it. Operate like a chess player, without necessarily adopting the social skills of one – think three moves ahead. Where is the conversation going? Where can you steer it?

Conversational do's

- Your surroundings. Every sales expert will tell you that one of the first steps to winning over your customer is having a shared experience.

Talking about what you both see is the best example of this; without any imagination needed, she's focusing on your words.

- What she's wearing. Every woman, unless she's naked, is giving you ready-made conversational pointers.

- Chick TV. Reality TV, soaps and celebrity culture are good, not just because it's more female dominated, but also because it's another form of connection, especially if you can take the piss out of it and she feels the same. You both know what the people you're talking about look and sound like, making it easier for her to concentrate on your words. Good storytelling abilities are attractive.

- A happy place. Most people have some fond memories of the town they grew up in, or at least something about their childhood, so probe about it. She'll feel happy, and come to associate this feeling with you.

Conversational don'ts

- Ex-girlfriends, especially if you hate them.

- Politics or religion. Nothing is more likely to

put off a girl than a bloke ranting on about taxes, asylum seekers or what God tells him every night. If she does ask you your political views, show a tolerant, live and let live attitude, as these views tend to be associated with successful men.

- Yourself. As the American statesman Benjamin Franklin once said, 'He that falls in love with himself will have no rivals.'

- Money. It's tacky to talk about how much you earn, and if you're well dressed and give off a confident air anyway, pointless.

- Family or private problems. Even if something she says leads easily into the topic of the sick mother you have to look after, you'll present yourself as a burden and a weakling.

Pheromones

Back in 1956 a team of German scientists made a strange discovery while experimenting on silkworms. Having scraped the glands off half a million female silkworms, they discovered that the smell of one particular secretion made all the male silkworms go crazy, in the same way a group of builders might do if a blonde in high heels walked by. They'd discovered pheromones, the chemical releases that make us horny and fall in love, and which teenaged boys buy from adverts in the back of magazines, in the hope of magically drawing women towards them.

Pheromones are naturally occurring scents used by the body as a signal to the opposite sex, and they're released in greater quantities when a human is in close proximity to a potential mate. Research has showed that all sorts of things can set them off, including, bizarrely, two people having the same taste in music. Why? It's all about connection.

Connection

Type 'spiritual connection' into Google and you'll find over 22 million results, which suggests that the act of creating a bond with another human being is quite important. And any connection between a man and a woman is more likely to make them want to mate, which is why couples often appear to look similar, whether they're dressed in matching track suits and baseball caps, or white make up, purple hair and black eye-liner.

Connecting is not just a matter of fashion taste, but of outlook and values, which is why you're on a hiding to nothing by going to venues that just aren't you. It's also the reason why a lot of mystical, new age stuff works so well on women (see 'Tricks'): in an increasingly selfish world where people fear being alone, not just physically but emotionally and spiritually, having a special bond with another person is quite a feat.

There are quite a few ways to form a connection.

- Physically. By touching.

- Outlook. If you're both disgusted by the venue, or a group of people in the corner, it shows you're on the same wavelength.

- Status. By showing you're the same attraction level, as most people at least marry men or women of equal attraction.

- Spiritually. By talking about 'chick crack', like tarot cards or astrology

- Taste. In music, fashion, TV or food.

Sometimes it might be one thing you say that makes her feel it; other times you have to work at it, by listening to what she says and looking out for keywords that reflect her views (any significant word you notice her repeating). The most obvious you'll hear in some people is 'spiritual', although it's probably the most vacuous-sounding word in the English language.

And having a similar experience also helps, which is why people often bring up the subject of TV programmes from childhood; even though there are six billion people in the world and the two of you were brought up maybe hundreds of miles apart, the fact that you may have watched the exact same show at the exact same time years go, and felt the exact same way about it, builds a connection between you. For the same reason nostalgic music from people's childhoods creates a bond in people the same age, one of the reasons for the success of the School Disco phenomenon.

Act hard to get

Buy her a drink, tell her how much you enjoy talking to her, but then say you have to head off in a minute because you've got other plans, or just ignore her briefly and start chatting to another woman. Having built you up as a possible mate in her mind, she'll suddenly wonder why you've lost interest, and may start to crave you like Dot Cotton craves cigarettes.

Make 'em laugh

During my time at *Nuts* I must have called hundreds of women and asked them what turns them on and what's the best way to get them into bed (something I'd be arrested for in any normal job). The number one answer they gave to the second question was 'make me laugh', but it's not enough in itself. Humour coupled with other qualities, namely confidence, will get you far; on its own it will not make a woman want to be anything more than just good friends.

Even top models laugh

As well as being a top model, Catherine McQueen is also a trained journalist and qualified lawyer. This is what she says about confident humour:

'I like people who are confident in themselves. It's a fine line, and don't try too hard, and if someone can make you laugh, you're interested; it doesn't matter about beer bellies, it's how the other person makes you feel. If they make you feel good, you want to be with them sub-consciously. You can be the quietest person in the room, but if you're quietly confident and sure of yourself, it doesn't matter.'

Good and bad humour

Never, ever use self-deprecating humour. Many people develop this kind of wit at school because it's the best way of getting bullies off your back, but you want a woman to sleep with you; while with bullies you just wanted them not to flush your head down the toilet, so a different approach is needed.

Even if a woman laughs at you taking the piss out of yourself for being useless with women, on a subconscious level she really will believe you're useless with women. On the other hand, don't belittle other people with bullying humour. It can be quite funny in the office but it's cruel, and a lot of women will think you're an insecure prick (which you probably are).

12

How to Flirt and Compliment

Flirting is universal to mankind, a way of testing the water before courtship or showing sexual availability in a harmless sort of way. The problem is that men and women flirt in different ways, and men are notoriously bad at picking up the signals.

Smiling

Most flirting is done with the eyes and the mouth, with a smile and a glance. Of course while every guide suggests you do that 'come to bed' look, not every man has it in him to pull it off, and much of the time we end up looking like a Thai transvestite. So don't force it, and don't even practise it. Just smile your normal smile, and maintain eye contact for two to three seconds when talking.

Winking

After you've shared a joke and both laughed, follow it up with a gentle but conspiratorial wink, a harmless platonic gesture but a special connection-forming one none the less. A wink says 'you and me, babe', without having to sound stupid by actually saying it.

Extended eye contact

Once you're in conversation with her, hold eye contact just a bit too long, so it's slightly uncomfortable. If she's embarrassed, and especially if she laughs nervously and blushes, it's probably time to check you're wearing your clean pair of underpants.

Teasing

A man and woman who are mutually attracted will most likely tease each other, perhaps about their clothes, an ugly ex or a sexual peccadillo. Sexual teasing is the most flirty of all, and only possible if you're chatting up a girl you know already. Teasing brings us all back to an infantile state of playfulness, the ideal mood for frolics to follow.

Checking her out

Contrary to what you were taught at school, (most) women like to be checked out by men, they just don't like feeling like a slab of meat being drooled at by a swivel-eyed drunk. Getting caught quickly glancing down will not do you any harm, assuming your tongue isn't hanging out or you're not sporting a lecherous foreign waiter stare. If she catches you, smile: you're appreciating her body, nothing more (obviously that's not the answer to give when her boyfriend shows up).

Nicknames

An original way of making a woman remember you is by giving her a nickname, something like 'shorty', 'little lady' or named after some moderately good-looking film star (if she's very good-looking) or a very good-looking one (if she's not). Alternatively, give her a Native

American name like 'She whose beauty could startle a rabbit.' She'll certainly remember you, at any rate.

Tickling

This is an advanced form of flirting, to be initiated only when you're confident she wants to play along. Ask her if she's ticklish – if she says yes, start to tickle her under the armpits; if she says no, challenge to prove her wrong by tickling her anyway. Because there are no erogenous zones involved, it's a safe form of pre-sex play-acting, but one that has sexual undertones.

Alex, a PR manager from London

'I knew one guy who was good-looking, funny and popular, but he fell down because he just wouldn't compliment women; maybe he thought it was false or he was embarrassed, but he had no luck with the ladies.'

Complimenting

We all love to be told we're great, and men are no different to women in that respect. And we all love to be around people who make us feel good about ourselves. So if you like a woman, tell her about her good points.

Women spend far more time and effort than us on getting dressed for work or an evening out, so thank them for their noble efforts that have made the office or bar a far more beautiful place to be. If you made that amount of effort at work on doing your job, you'd expect some praise or recognition from your colleagues. In fact you'd be pretty pissed off if they didn't notice.

Women also spend a lot of money on their clothes and fret about whether something matches or makes them look slim, (while a bad item of clothing, not to mention a crap haircut, can ruin her confidence and make her feel like all her tax return days have come at once). So when a man appreciates the effort she has gone to it will not just brighten up her day, but make him welcome in her circle of friends any time.

The best compliments are about clothes and hair, then, but it's not enough to just say 'nice clothes', it has to be something specific. Study what a woman is wearing. Make a note of the colour scheme, the accessories, and think what she is trying to do. What statement is she making? Does she want to look bohemian, clever or tall? Study every woman you see in the street – it only takes a split second and you shouldn't get caught. Try not to wear night vision goggles and a balaclava.

If she's wearing something interesting or an item that looks like it has a story attached, ask about it; she'll be impressed by how inquisitive you are, and it sets off endless conversational possibilities.

Be careful about the weight issue, for God's sake. Never say, 'That makes you look slim,' as she'll register that as, 'So I look fat normally?' Those sorts of comments are for close friends only.

And if she compliments you, accept it gracefully and say, 'Thank you, you're very sweet.' Don't deny it or worse, brush it aside as if she's being dishonest.

An exercise

At work tomorrow morning practise by complimenting three different women on something they're wearing or have done with their hair. You'll be amazed at how differently they treat you, and you may even get a cup of tea out of it.

13

Body Language

How often has a loud mouth friend of yours said, 'She was right into me,' after a woman has almost vomited in his face? But just as often we go away lamenting that she wasn't interested when the woman was practically sticking her tongue in our ear. Body language is a science, and people who master it can earn good money in the area of law enforcement, the military and sales.

Loads of people claim to be body language experts, especially those men who think every woman in the world fancies them, but the truth is that people react differently. Having said that, there are signs that a woman is interested, even if she's not consciously aware she's doing it, and having a basic knowledge of the subject will help your confidence and stop you wasting time on women who clearly aren't interested.

Signs of availability

When a body language expert walks into a bar, he'll know instantly which women are single and interested, and which will be either attached or simply not in the mood.

Firstly available women will be sitting close to the most social areas of the venue, such as the bar or central area, and they'll have a good view of the surroundings and especially the entrance. If she's chosen a location with a good lookout spot, either she's interested in a new sexual partner, or she's a spy; either option makes her interesting. And ignore the clothes she's wearing, as many a happily engaged woman likes to dress raunchily on a night out; instead look for these:

- Standing with legs apart and her weight on only one foot.

- Playing with any cylindrical object, most likely the stem of a wine glass.

- Slowly crossing and uncrossing her legs, especially if an interested man is watching her.

- Displaying legs crossed closely together and intertwined. When a woman does this she reproduces the intense muscle activity the legs show before and during sex, which explains why men are like moths to lamps when they lay eyes on this simple gesture.

Calibrating

Once you've started a conversation, you'll want to know what signs to look out for, so you don't badly misread the signals and, in her mind, ruin a perfectly nice chat between two people by sticking your tongue down her throat. Tony Clink has a method of testing a woman's reactions that he calls 'calibrating'.

We all know that different women give off different, often mixed signals; their nose might twitch if unhappy, or maybe they'll scratch their cheek. So early on in the conversation ask her to describe a really happy moment in her life, and an unhappy one; remembering the way her face and body react when describing these highs and lows, so you'll know whether you're going in the right direction in future.

But remember to still focus on the conversation, and don't end up staring at her hands or neck looking for signals – you'll look very weird.

Positive signals

- Facing towards you, especially her feet, knees and legs.

- Tilting her head.

- Leaning forward.

- Echoing you (see below).

- Playing with her neck, almost as if to draw attention to it (the neck is an erogenous zone and also the easiest giveaway to someone's age).

- Subconsciously trying to look more feminine, like drawing her legs in to appear smaller or crossing and uncrossing her legs to draw attention to them (and no, not like Sharon Stone). Men do a similar thing by trying to look more masculine, such as expanding their chests and raising their shoulders.

- Dilated, larger pupils (though she might just be on Class A drugs).

- Looking at you with half-closed eyelids (though she might be on Class B drugs).

- Showing signs of nerves when you look her way.

- Tossing hair away from her face or over her shoulder.

- Sideways glances.

- Licking her lips, or pouting.

- Exposing shoulders or wrists.

- Best of all – if she dangles her shoe while talking to you.

Of course there are so many possible signals that it might seem impossible to talk to any woman without her giving off at least one – be warned that some are just signs of comfort and warmth, and not sexual attraction, while some negative signs could just be nerves. However, if you notice at least three or four, you can be fairly confident that it's on.

Negative signals

- Body facing away from you

- Arms crossed

- Blocking her body from you, with folded arms, drink held defensively

- Rolling her eyes

Postural echo

Have you ever looked at two very good friends talking, or two strangers who've really hit it off? They'll grab their waists in an identical way, hold their drinks exactly the same, and fold their legs like they're part of a dance routine. This is a physical sign of empathy. Anthropologists call it 'postural congruence' or 'postural echo.' But mirroring, as it's sometimes called, also creates trust, as well as reflecting it, as any salesman knows; it's a symptom as well as a cause of warmth and security.

So by simply paying attention to a woman's body movements, you can use them to make her feel more relaxed and comfortable in your presence, and therefore increase your chances later on.

Begin by watching out for when she takes her breaths, while obviously avoiding looking at her chest, and start to synchronise your breathing – from this all will naturally follow. Keeping your eye on the conversation, subtly copy how she holds herself and smile when she smiles. If she taps the table or floor with one part of the body, you do it with another part, but at the same pace. This is called pacing by practitioners of NLP – Neuro-Linguistic Programming – the form of psychology used in Ross Jeffries' speed seduction (more about this in 'Tricks'). After pacing for several minutes, change your pace and see if she follows; if not, go back to following her rhythm and try again when she seems more comfortable with you.

135

Space

Humans are territorial by nature and have personal distances in which they feel comfortable and those in which they feel threatened. These may vary according to culture, but wherever you're from, you'll want to remain at different distances from strangers, acquaintances, friends and intimates.

Having a good understanding of body space is a very useful skill when chatting up a woman. If you want to make a move, then you have to enter into her intimate space at the right time, without making her feel threatened or invaded. For example, when you first approach a woman or talk to her in a group, you're in the very non-threatening social zone, something we can share willingly with dozens of strangers every day.

When you progress past initial small talk and go into the chat-up proper, you're moving into the personal zone. From this point both of you have your full attention on each other.

These rules obviously go out of the window if you're in a crowded pub or club where everyone is forced into each other's space (it's also in venues like this where most violence occurs, as men feel more threatened). But make sure you've spent a reasonable time in the personal zone before you make a move; nothing puts a woman off like a lunge.

Spatial Awareness

'Proxemics' is the study of spatial relationships between people, and was recognised as a field in its own right in the 1960s. As well as dealing with love and intimacy, space is also a crucial factor in aggression and violence; when typically starting a fight, the first thing a man will do is to violate his opponent's space, often by moving his head very close. In the same way police interrogators found that they could unnerve suspects simply by getting extremely close to them; this had more of an impact than shouting 'you're going down, son,' 'Shut it!' or even 'look here you slag, spill the beans.'

- **Public zone** (12 ft or more)
  The distance with which we feel safe with strangers; private talking is obviously not possible, but neither is physical attack nor catching any disease. If a woman insists on staying this far away from you, you have serious groundwork to do.

- **Social zone** (4 ft to12 ft)
  Social conversation between acquaintances or colleagues, or the distance we like to keep in a group situation.

- **Personal zone** (18 inches to 4 ft)
  The distance you keep with friends, or for a one-on-one conversation. You would not feel comfortable at this distance with someone you did not like or trust.

- **Intimate zone** (up to 18 inches)
  The area for kissing or whispering, where
  you only let lovers or very good friends; you
  would feel very uncomfortable if anyone else
  came this close to you.

Open up

When you're talking to someone really boring and making a hell of an effort to look interested, your body language will usually give away your true feelings. This is called 'non-verbal leakage', and the most common sign is when your head is facing them but the body is turned away. If you're a naturally shy or defensive person you may be giving out this signal to women you like, so be careful, because she'll probably pick up on it.

Don't be scared to open up your body language; being a shrivelled shrimp of a man will not endear you to women, and don't be afraid to be touched. Study politicians when you see them at functions – they train their whole lives to make themselves look interested when forced to talk to some inarticulate rat boy at a community centre when they'd rather be dining with mysterious foreign businessmen.

Don't fidget

Even if you talk like the sort of man who knows what he wants from life and to hell with those pen-pushers in city hall, your body might still give you away as a nervous wreck, so be careful not to fidget, stare at your shoes or stand with pigeon feet. A confident man stands legs apart, with expansive arms (this shows generosity as well as strength) and with his chest stuck out, though without looking like a gorilla.

Give her the signals

You want the woman to know you're interested in her, right?

- Make sure your body isn't shielding you from her by talking to her side-on.

- Stand with your hands on your hips, accentuating your masculinity.

- Lightly stroke the outside of your thigh while talking to her.

- Flatten your hair with the palm or, if you're wearing a tie, straighten it.

- Tuck your belly in.

Touch her

A common mistake men make is to think that just because a girl likes to touch you, she's desperate to engage in some unnatural carnal acts banned in most George Bush-voting US states. But while some women are innocently tactile, that's not to say that the very act of body contact – on the shoulder, elbow, hand or knee – doesn't help the seduction process; if a woman feels comfortable about physical contact with you, you've broken down one barrier, and men should always use the chance to use a non-sexual touch to make a woman feel better about more intimate contact.

Firstly, make the effort to shake hands when you meet. Some people like to go for a kiss on the cheek, but frankly I always find this a bit weird with someone you've just met; there are no set rules about this, but generally in Britain only friends should kiss, unless you work in the fashion industry or Mafia.

Once you've established a rapport, follow up a compliment or successful joke with a tap of her elbow. This is the least sexual part of the human body (although somewhere out there some weirdo probably gets a kick from having it rubbed), so it makes the ideal starting point.

You might worry that she feels you're coming on too strong, but this is usually quite easy to see – she won't smile and her body will adopt a defensive posture, shrunken with vital organs covered.

If not, then you've gone a long way to making her feel at ease with physical contact. Next try the shoulder and, for fiendish level body contact, when you're sitting down, the knee. It goes without saying that you should never touch a woman's breasts, unless invited to.

How to look her into bed

As well as maintaining good eye-contact, look from eye to eye, and then down at her lips when she's talking. The lips are the most erogenous zone of the face so by looking at hers, she'll be drawn towards yours. Try this in an ordinary environment, and see if you don't pick up good signals as a result.

One-on-one

Sustained eye contact in a one-on-one situation at a party or pub doesn't just show that you're confident and honest: it tells the woman that she's the only person in the world right now as far as you're concerned. Looking over a woman's shoulders while talking gives the impression of incredible arrogance, and makes you look like a shark who's after the next bunk-up. Sometimes when you're chatting up a woman you rate at around a six or seven an unbelievably stunning nine or ten will walk past, almost as if sent by Satan to test your resolve. Resist with all your strength the opportunity to gawp, especially if she has 95 per cent of her breasts on show. Women always pick up on these things with the sort of radar that makes a whale's navigational system seem primitive in comparison.

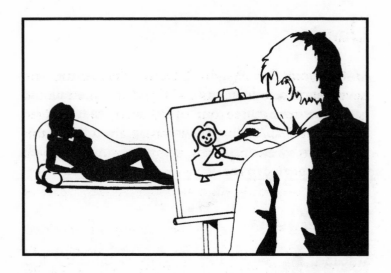

14

Tricks

You don't necessarily just need to have what employers call 'soft skills', i.e. charm and wit. Some men go that little bit further and learn to do something to entertain the ladies. So remember the Boy Band Theory – no group is complete without an entertainer.

Dancing

Unless your dad is John Travolta, chances are you never learned to dance as a kid, and few men would get more than three out of 30 were they judged by a *Come Dancing* panel. It wasn't always like this – time was when men were taught to move, and you wouldn't get by in society without some knowledge. Before house parties and alcopops, it was a part of the courting ritual.

Dancing is the oldest art form, the most primitive, and the most sexual. Whether it's the Charleston or bumping and grinding, sex lies at its origins, it's just that more cautious societies have tried their best to filter out the sexuality to make it safe.

If a man is good at one then he's good at the other. Not my words, but those of every woman on earth.

But even if you have been blessed with all the natural cool of Prince Charles at a dancehall reggae gig, then it's better to make a prat of yourself than not dance at all. Dancing terribly is always better than sulking by the side like an idiot, and sometimes the worse the better, as long as you can do it with an idiotic smile on your face. Think of Sacha Baron Cohen's camp Austrian character Bruno – if it makes us laugh, it's going to do the same for women.

Alternatively, go to dance classes with a female friend, where as a man you'll be met with the same enthusiasm as a washed up crate of lager by a group of Royal Navy sailors on a desert island. Never mind that you're cringingly awful and all the women are leering at the Cuban dance instructor; they'll be impressed that you bothered to come at all. And dancing is not entirely about natural rhythm, although that helps; there are some basic rules that you can learn that will increase your potential no end.

Chick crack

Astrology, tarot cards and palm reading: all total and utter crap, but just as many men believe that there are aliens living in New Mexico or the Pentagon just had a gas leak that day, a lot of women go for mind, bollocks and spirit. Just take a day off work and look at some of the crap spewing out from daytime TV, such as horoscopes, psychic readings and contacting the dead: it's the female equivalent of porn.

Women, and a lot of men for that matter, hate the idea that we're just sex robots biologically programmed to mate with a suitable partner for the purpose or having children. Where's the romance in that? The poem 'Let me count the ways I love thee' didn't continue with 'your symmetrical face suggests any potential offspring would be effective in resisting illness.' That's the role astrology plays – if you tell a Virgo woman that she's destined to fall for an Aquarius man, then that creates the tingly feeling we all call love.

Palm reading

This is especially effective because it gives you the chance to touch hands and, providing you're not covered in a clammy sweat, connect with her emotionally. It also allows you to make some corny line about a disruption in her love line 'right about now'; just don't suggest that her life line points to an imminent, tragic end.

The basics of palmistry are simple. Look at your right hand and you'll see two horizontal and two vertical lines: on most people's palms, these meet to form a rough 'm' shape. The horizontals are the heart and the head/brain line, which indicate how we feel and think; the others are the fate and life line, which relate to our life force. A thick heart line suggest a greater urge to love and connect, and this is the best 'analysis' to use, unless the girl fancies herself as an intellectual, in which case use the length of her head line to suggest she wants to challenge herself more.

There is, of course, a great deal more to it than that, and there are plenty of books available if you wish to study up on the subject.

Handwriting analysis

Women love extrasensory perception (ESP), the basis of chick crack; as impressive as the likes of Derren Brown are to all of us, their powers are especially seductive to women. And though we might not have Mr Brown's powers, we can try.

Handwriting analysis is simple, fun and can give you strange supernatural powers.

All you do is go up to a woman and say you've got a pack of cards that can analyse her handwriting and ask her if she'd like to try it out. The Grapho-Deck ®, as it's called, contains 56 cards that match up squiggles to personality traits, and is a great practical gimmick to bring to the pub. You can find them on eBay.

But you don't even need any props: as many TV shows have proven, you can tell a person things about them that seem unnervingly accurate, yet they apply to everyone in the entire world. This is called 'cold reading' (or the 'Barnum Effect' after the 19th century showman), and it simply involves generic statements such as:

- 'You are sometimes anxious around people you don't know.'

- 'You are having problems with a friend.'

- 'You find your job unsatisfying.'

- 'You have a box of unsorted photos at home.'

All of which are generic enough to be universal, but said with enough mystique, and in the right atmosphere, you should have her saying, 'That's so true – that's just like me!'

Alternatively tell her your graphological powers work best with numeric figures, and ask her to write down her telephone number for you to study, then say, 'Thanks, I'll call you Monday,' and leave.

Reflexology

Learn to give good foot and hand massages; if you get a reputation as the man who makes people's feet feel great by taking out the tension, women will be over you like ducks to a piece of bread.

Magic tricks

'Everyone is impressed by someone who can do something, and compared to music or something similar, you don't have to carry anything around with street magic.' So says Paul Zenon, Britain's number one street magician. I once interviewed Paul in Brighton, where a photographer and I followed him around as he went up to women and tried to get their phone numbers by impressing them with magic tricks. He got ten in an hour and a half, which is not a bad result even for the famously debauched seaside town.

There is little doubt that learning a bit of magic is no bad thing. 'It's all to do with that initial contact,' he explains. 'If you try the cold approach to women where you just wander up, they have their guard up because they're expecting a cheesy chat-up line. But if you've got something to do, it's almost a form of misdirection. The thing about a trick is that it's something visual, and if you ain't an oil painting, it's just as well they've got something to look at. Once they've got hold of something that belongs to you, or vice versa, they've got a reason to stay.'

It's also a handy way of initiation physical contact. 'Because you're using props, it's a good excuse to grab their hands in a nice way, because if you just physically touch them for no reason, that's quite intimidating.'

Business cards

Business cards are cheap, yet a sensible-looking, well-designed card will make her believe you're a successful high-ranking male. But if you're sharking around student bars or on a lad's holiday, for about a fiver you can make a load of stupid ones with 'Kiss Me Hardly' or 'International playboy, Paris, New York, Merthyr Tydfil'. Rather than going up to a woman and saying, 'Here's my card,' give her yours after she's given you her number – at least she'll know you're either vaguely ambitious or, in the latter case, possessing a sense of humour.

Art

One of the best routines of American seduction guru Ross Jeffries involves that old cheesy ploy of asking if a woman if he can draw a portrait of her. Women generally say yes to this (who wouldn't?), so he spends a few minutes appearing to put an incredible amount of effort into his work, only to present her with a childish stick-drawing interpretation. It's bound to raise a laugh.

Guitars

Learn to play an instrument, and make it the acoustic guitar. You need only to know about three chords to play a simple love song, and as long as a house party venue has one, you're sorted for the evening. Why?

Look at peacocks. Evolution experts love them, mainly because they don't make sense. Peacocks, unlike the female of the species (peahens), have bright, ostentatious dazzling multi-coloured tails that are a massive disadvantage in the natural world. In fact it's positively daft, because even the dimmest predator with wonky eyes could spot them a mile away – it would be like the army providing its soldiers with dayglo orange leotard uniforms. These plumes exist for no other reason than that the peahens like them, so that over millions of years peacocks have developed brighter and louder and stupider-looking tails.

Men evolved artistic ability, especially music, for exactly the same reasons; they serve no purpose other than to attract women. It's called sexual selection, which is why men who can play the guitar will never go home alone.

Poetry

Start reciting romantic poetry to a woman, and chances are she'll either think you're a total nutter, or the sexiest, most romantic man since Colin Firth emerged out of that lake with a wet frilly shirt. Look up the works of

Elizabeth Barrett Browning, W. H. Auden, Lord Bryon and, of course, William Shakespeare.

Dogs

He's not called man's best friend just because he rescues stranded climbers and even has the decency to bring along a small case of brandy. A dog is the best gimmick of all for when you're out looking for love, though obviously I wouldn't recommend getting one purely for that purpose. But if you do need a pulling partner, dump your human mates and instead ask to borrow one of their dogs; he won't put you down, go for the same girl, or bring up any embarrassing past incidents. Never turn down the chance to walk a friend's mutt.

Flowers

A far more direct route is to buy flowers (there's usually some bloke hanging around in most city centres) and present them as a token of your appreciation. Make it look like a selfless gesture and don't ask if you can join her; simply tell her she's beautiful and should be told so regularly (this is less likely to work on very attractive girls).

Speed seduction

Wiry, balding and slightly geeky-looking, Ross Jeffries is,

by his own admission, not a natural born lady-killer. Yet to 60,000 followers, he is part modern day Casanova and part guru, founder of a massive, worldwide movement that claims to have turned the art of attraction into a science. Jeffries and his 'speed seduction' theory, which uses suggestion and word 'patterns' to arouse women, has led to a multimillion-dollar industry of books, CDs and self-help seminars, spawning imitators and rivals galore.

Speed seduction works by using Neuro-Linguistic Programming (NLP), a form of mild hypnotism that grew out of the post-hippy growth of 'personal development' (yes I know what you're thinking, only in America). NLP is based on the theory that our beliefs, feelings and sense of reality can all be shaped by verbal suggestion, and is used in sports coaching, therapy and business management.

Studying what caused lust and attraction in women, he developed a series of hypnotic 'patterns,' commands disguised in normal conversation that would make the speaker irresistible to the opposite sex.

Ross's method is to 'unlock her imagination,' by getting a woman to imagine her perfect situation, then by using patterns he builds up feelings of arousal. In speed seduction, one would innocently start to describe a hugely pleasurable experience, whether a rollercoaster ride or a fantastic meal, but all the time working her up into a frenzy of pleasure by mere suggestion, and at appropriate moments making subtle pointing gestures at yourself. Along the way Jeffries introduces 'weasel phrases', subconsciously geared towards enticing a woman into finding him sexually attractive. The ultimate purpose of this patterning is to make a woman think about her happiest and most ecstatic moments and link those feelings to the man doing the speaking.

And despite many imitators and rivals, Jeffries remains number one, and today charges over $1195 per head at his seminars, where he repeats mantras like, 'Don't spend money on a woman until you have slept with her,' 'Don't be a loser,' and 'This will get you laid more than a Porsche or a kilo of coke.' And he even has a money-back guarantee: 'You don't get laid, I don't get paid.'

He also claims to be the inspiration for Frank T. J. Mackey, Tom Cruise's character in *Magnolia*, who's best remembered for the catchphrase: 'Respect the cock!'

The seduction community

As a result of Jeffries' work, a worldwide 'seduction community' has emerged, a web-based association of 'pick-up artists' who follow either Jeffries or other players, such as journalist-turned-player Neil Strauss, Tony Clink, David DeAngelo or Eric 'Mystery' von Markovik – 'The World's Greatest Pick-up Artist'.

PUAs (everything is turned into an acronym, and with a massive glossary PUAs often seem to have a language of their own) see seduction as a science, not an art, claiming that there are basic laws that allow one man to turn from geek to love god.

Neil Strauss' best-selling book *The Game* caused

uproar when it was published in 2005, recounting his transformation from sexually unsuccessful writer into the 'Jedi' of PUAs. Using the name 'Style', Strauss learned all the tricks of the 'Mystery Method' and, a year after starting out, was living in a Hollywood mansion, dating 10 different 'HB10s' (hot babes who rate 10/10, or stunners in English) and convincing rival girlfriends to have threesomes with him.

The Mystery Method, named after Eric von Markovik (aka 'Mystery'), a 6'5' Canadian magic enthusiast is all about acquiring the six qualities of alpha males – confidence, a smile, good grooming, a sense of humour, the ability to connect with people, and being the centre of the room. In fact all of the seduction philosophy comes from the writing of geneticists such as Richard Dawkins and Matt Ridley, who would be bemused to find they are worshipped by Californian serial seducers.

Using these, Strauss and a whole load of other geek-turned-womanisers were able to become the rock stars of seduction. Soon thousands of men were communicating via websites such as FastSeduction.com, and in other 'lairs' where they boasted and exchanged tips. The seduction community incorporated men from all walks of life, and soon developed a cultish quality.

15

Niche Markets

Internet dating

Only five years ago Internet dating was still seen as a fringe affair where you'd must likely hook up with weirdos, German penis-eating cannibals, or that woman in America who turned out to have her dead husband in the freezer. Now, with millions of single men and women using it around the world, Internet dating has become mainstream, acceptable and for some a replacement for conventional dating. Over 50 per cent of people (in the US and UK) in the dating game use the Internet, so that in 30 years time half of the nation's kids will owe their existence to a company like match.com.

I spoke to a man who has a lot of experience in the area – Pete Cashmore, a journalist at *Nuts*, who has met about 100 women on the Internet over the last five years, and estimates he has known 20 in the biblical sense. 'The reason I started was I went to a dinner party where there were just eight couples, and me; and I thought, "This is crap." London is an unforgiving place, but by going on the Internet you're taking control of your destiny.'

Making a profile

'To start with you have to write your own profile. What you're interested in, what newspapers you read, your favourite authors and where you go on holiday. It's very interesting because in some you're given a multiple choice: What's your favourite book? Is it *About A Boy* or *Angela's Ashes*?'

Some Internet dating guides suggest reading other men's profiles to have a look at what is successful, but Pete thinks otherwise. 'I thought that way lies damnation. I know a lot of girls do, and they get incredibly vicious and catty about it, so I didn't want to be thinking "What's he got that I haven't?" if a very similar profile got dates and I didn't.'

Be yourself

Humour is the best option, light-hearted and non-threatening. 'What I discovered fairly early on is that people lie about themselves a lot, so it's not worth just picking the sort of interests women will like, much better to be funny; being amusing on the site is very valued.'

Making an approach

'Their main fear is that you're either a weirdo, or a rapist, or both, so that's the main hurdle. You have to make clear straightaway that you're not. Always try to make your message funny when you e-mail a woman, and don't make sexual references. There's a fine line between flirty, and sounding like a horrible old letch. But one line I've always used is to say that someone has really nice hair.

'The ratio on most sites is far more men to women, and in probably two-thirds of dates I've done the asking. On some sites they give you options where you can sort of declare interest without sending someone a message, on match.com you can send them a wink, while on another you can send them a smiley, and on DatingDirect.com you can add someone to your friends list, and see who's added you to theirs. Once that happens you can make the first step.'

Don't carpet bomb

Some men send hundreds of almost identical e-mails out, but as with any dating, the key is to target a particular market. 'Because of the ratio, a good-looking man might get a trickle of interest, while women will just get blitzed in the first week they join by men who carpet bomb new people with almost identical copied and pasted e-mails, in the hope that someone will respond. It's not worth doing. In my experience you can always tell the ones that are copied because there's almost nothing there that relates specifically to something you say.

'In my profile I think I'm actually giving anyone contacting me a lot of material and so when they just copy someone else's e-mails, then in my view they're only a step up from a spam e-mail that reads, 'Hello I am Zlottie from St. Petersburg, I want to make happy husband, please send me £170 air fare.' It's the personal touches that actually get you dates, so I'm not a copier and paster.'

Posting a photo

'Obviously I put up a grossly inaccurate picture of myself, and once I get e-mailing start sending them more realistic ones, inching them to reality. I met one girl who must have been two stone heavier than her photo suggested, and she wasn't a tall girl, so I feel in those situations you have the right to be rude because they've been dishonest. There was an occasion where I made the mistake of seeing one who hadn't put up her photo, who'd said "I consider myself very attractive." Which is all very well, but from an empirical point of view, she was the least attractive human being I've ever met.'

The date

'Take them to a nice pub, or relaxed bar, and don't go over the top, because this is not the same as a normal date. When you meet her, get a drink. After the third drink, and I shouldn't even say this because it's trade secret, turn to her and say, 'I always like to give someone the opportunity to call it a night.' By this stage she will have made her mind up, and if she wants to stick around, that means she likes you. You couldn't do that on a normal date.'

Recommended sites:
match.com
DatingDirect.com
LoveandFriends.com
SpeedDater.co.uk
udate.com

Speed dating

Speed dating is where a group of about 15 men and 15 women (but always an equal number) pay to go to a venue in the hope of meeting a partner. The women stay seated all night, while the men move around and get three minutes of talk with each; at the end everyone fills out a card where they say who they liked and, if there is a match, the organisers will arrange a date. Strangely enough, it was invented by a New York rabbi in 1999 as a way of getting young Jewish people to get together.

The pitfalls of speed dating are many; it's firstly very embarrassing, very stressful, at least the first time, and there's always the feeling that this is a bit like publicising your desperation. So it's vital to present an air of laid back, cool, 'Hey, I just did this for a laugh' nonchalance; and don't give the impression you're looking for a wife.

Bear in mind that the women you talk to are going to be asked a lot of questions, so keep them original.

Don't say:

- And what do you do?

- Why are you speed dating?

- What's your favourite film, band, song etc?

Instead, ask her how her day was, where she got her outfit and where does she want to be in ten years time.

Do some research on the demographics of the speed dating night you're going to; some areas attract particular industries, so if you're night has a reputation for being full of PR girls, buy one of the PR industry's magazines or websites; people are always impressed if you, a layman, know a bit about their world.

You only have three minutes to impress the girl, which is just about two statements and two questions, so be original, and be quick.

But don't be rushed, even though it is only three minutes; while speed dating nights give e-mail details of mutually compatible couples, a lot of them just turn into big piss-ups afterwards, where you'll have a much better chance of striking it lucky.

Other normal dating tips apply, including:

- Make eye contact

- Don't slouch

- Don't appear arrogant

- Make an effort with your clothes

- Keep your arms open

- Compliment her on her clothes

- Keep the conversation light, and not sleazy

- And smile

Remember – anything that makes you cringe with embarrassment can only be a good thing for your pulling skills.

In a speed dater's words:
'You won't be up against much competition, as these evenings appear to be dominated by nervy I.T. nerds, sleazeball wannabe Lotharios and assorted other social misfits – many of whom lie pathetically about their age. Some of the women there were very nice; plenty of teachers, nurses and assorted others who rarely meet young, single men in their workplace. And the "drinks" after the actual event itself regularly turns into a booze-fuelled knocking-shop.' **Richard, Norfolk**

Older women

If you're after an older woman who will teach you the ways of the world and have her own flat to boot, you can either try two approaches: try to meet on her own level, or be her toy boy.

The first is a lot harder, because if there's a fair age difference (over 10 years), the gulf in your experience, upbringing and financial situation will be massive, and she won't want a younger man who thinks he's as learned and world-weary as she is. Let her have the edge in these areas.

She won't go for you for your sophistication or experience, so emphasise the strength of youth: energy, fitness, stamina and playfulness. Make it clear you don't want to be serious, because she will be well aware that it's not going to last. But use your charm and youthful looks to your advantage, and flatter her that she can still turns heads far younger than hers by telling her how sexy she is.

But don't be immature; older women are more accepting of faults (some might say less picky), but childish behaviour will just annoy her.

And always remove at least seven years when guessing her age.

Foreigners

Depending on where they're from, foreign women will have come to Britain with a romantic image of Englishmen, Scotsmen, Irishmen and Welshmen, so play up to it. If they're coming here with a romance in mind, sell them your national image:

- Humour

- Your sense of history
  (especially with Americans)

- Sophistication
  (especially Australians and French girls)

- Reserved dignity, but in a good way
  (especially with Americans)

But avoid the negative image our countries have:

- Badly dressed

- Sly

- Unfriendly

- Unromantic

- Most of all, drunk

Larger city centres, especially London, are filled with foreign girls, so a bit of geographical research is in order. Find out at least one funny fact about a country, so that when you come to meet one of its daughters, you'll be ready with a funny line.

And feel free to betray your country: I had a friend who pulled an Argentinean by telling her they should have the Falklands.

Captive audiences

Barmaids and waitresses are both harder and easier to pull than other women. They're talking to you, and approachable, which is a bonus, but if they're attractive they probably get asked out every day, and have heard every line in the book.

Be polite and respectful. Remember that many men, especially if they make a buck or two, look down at anyone serving them and will act in an arrogant manner. Because of this barmaids hate arrogance even more than other women, so be polite and confident, but not smarmy.

Try to avoid being cheesy, as well; of course you should do this anyway, but you're dealing with women who get asked out more than most, so you'll need a different tactic. Maybe it's offering your good knowledge of the city, as many barmaids are from out of town.

Don't pressure her. Make your interest known, but make it clear you want to see her out of hours and you're not going to hassle her at work. She's doing a job, trying to make a living for herself, so she doesn't have the option of walking away from you unless the landlord kicks you out. Tell her about a good after hours place that you and your friends are moving onto, and invite her along; she'll want to relax after a hard shift dealing with people like you.

With waitresses it's more difficult because the atmosphere is less boozy and fun. If you're by yourself, bring some work with you so you look busy and not like someone who's just killing time. Always go between 3 and 6 pm, when it is fairly relaxed, and choose a moment when she's not manically busy, and just ask for her number. You haven't got time to make small talk, so simply explain that you appreciate she's busy but you'd like to see her for a coffee or drink after work some time, and that her answer won't affect the tip you give her.

16

Making a Move

So you've approached a woman, talked, flirted, connected and assured her that you're not a mentalist. You're now in front of goal, and the keeper's had a heavy night on the sauce – it's simple to put the ball in the net. Though this should in fact be the easiest part of the night, a lot of men are self-assured with the initial approach and charm offensive, but lose their nerve when it comes to the big stage. Chokers, as they're called in tennis.

There are different ways of sealing the deal; you can either ask for a phone number, or move in straight away. First you have to get her alone.

Separating from the pack

Again I wouldn't follow the hunting metaphors too closely, not just for moral reasons but because animals like to separate the weakest prey from the herd, while you're trying to get the healthiest and best looking.

Getting a woman away from her friends is a lot easier if she's keen on you to start with; it also helps if she's in a smallish group, but if there's just one other she won't want to leave her alone (unless your friend is taking one from the team), while in a bigger group she may be more self-conscious about getting a reputation (depending on what kind of friends she has, and how hazy the night is – a lot of things can get lost in the fog of drink).

In a moderately busy bar, groups of two or three women are best, but in big night clubs where everyone's pissed and gets lost, bigger groups are more likely to be up for it.

In a club asking her to dance is a good removal technique, although the downside is you'll need to be able to dance; in a pub you can ask to play her at pool; alternatively now is the time to offer to buy her a drink. In Ireland and Scotland, and soon in England and Wales, asking her to join you for a cigarette outside is a non-healthy option.

If none of these exits is available, tell her that you have to rejoin your friends (assuming they haven't come over or have drifted back) and that you'd like her to meet them, inventing some tenuous reason for an introduction, such as one of your friends sharing an interest or profession (make sure your pal is well trained not to start getting in your way). Alternatively tell her that you have to go (being busy and wanted is always an attractive trait) but that you'd like to see her again, and ask how that would be possible. At this stage she should offer you her phone number.

Of course if you have a good wingman, by this stage he should have done in his job in keeping her friend or the rest of the group occupied.

Signs of interest

- It helps to know whether you have a chance. If she's at all interested in you, she'll make it clear even when she's not making it obvious.

- She asks your name before you've offered it.

- She asks if you have a girlfriend.

- She stays with you even when her friends go off somewhere.

- You go to the toilet and she's still there when you come back.

- When you tell her you have to go soon, she asks where.

- She laughs even if she disagrees with you, or laughs at pretty much anything you say.

Fact: 10.48 pm is officially the best time to pull, according to question-answering SMS service AQA; perhaps it's something to do with the rush to the bar.

How to kiss

Once you have laid the groundwork, making a move is easy. First ensure that:

- You have privacy, away from her friends.

- You're in the personal zone already.

- Some form of body contact has already taken place.

- You've picked up verbal and physical signs of interest.

After you've ticked that check list, it's simply a matter of closing the body language until you're facing (dance floors are the best place for this), upping the flirting stakes while allowing more frequent and longer pauses in the conversation, and slowly moving into the intimate zone. This is now what's known as an open goal and, short of natural disaster or the sudden appearance of your mother or her ex-boyfriend, you're there.

And don't start off with a great big cow's lick: gentle kisses on the lips are the order of the day, followed by something more full-on.

How to ask for a date

Getting a date is surprisingly easy once you gain even a tiny bit of confidence. Surveys have shown that more than 80 per cent of single women will agree to a date assuming that the man doesn't seem weird or dangerous, and if you have this air then you really have serious problems. A date is just a one off for her and carries no promise whatsoever; she won't gain a sluttish reputation for going for a drink, and the chances are you'll pay for most of it. Beside which, women like the whole window-shopping nature of the mating game almost as much as they like shopping itself, so she probably just thinks of you as an interesting-looking dress that might just fit.

So as the saying goes, 'If you don't ask, you don't get', and never be afraid to ask a woman for a telephone number or to meet one night after work. Regret is far harder to live with than rejection; one can torment you for years, the other is forgotten in hours.

Don't be vague, by saying, 'Would you like to go out some time?' Be specific and know what day and event you want. Wednesday and Thursday are best, as they aren't as intrusive as the weekends. Beside which, you want to give the impression you're busy, remember? Busy this weekend jumping out of a plane in Afghanistan or partying on Roman Abramovich's yacht.

Or instead of asking openly for her number, say you'd love to meet some time – if she likes you, she'll give her number or at the very least an e-mail address.

Take the initiative

No amount of changes in the workplace or parliamentary laws are ever going to alter the fact that we do the vast amount of asking out. But don't for a minute think that women are passive in the whole process; they're choosing dates just as much as a company advertises for and selects a new applicant for a job.

So never ever offer a woman your number without getting hers; most of the time she won't call. Even if she likes you, she'll think you're gutless.

And make a timely exit once you've secured the number. Leave the audience wanting more, as showbiz types say.

How to arrange a date

It's far, far better to arrange the date in person and ring just to confirm, rather than simply getting a number and calling to set it up: a telephone call will be far more awkward than chatting, face-to-face, in a lively environment, and setting a night makes it more difficult for her to back out. So always have handy possible dates ready; build up an internal database of good restaurants in town, nice bars, and other interesting venues. If she says no to your offer but doesn't offer an alternative date and still gives her phone number, she could be leading you on; make it clear that you want a confirmed date before you call, because you're a busy man, but that you would like to see her again. Carry a diary if you think it will help you seem busier.

Making the call

Timing is everything. Call when you say you will, but not at the exact moment, as it will feel too regimented and fake. Don't let the moment pass, though, as your confidence will drop as the pressure builds – far better to call a bit earlier. And if you said you'd call on Sunday afternoon, don't ponder it – pick up the phone without thinking when you feel the nerve come to you – just as you did when you first approached her.

Some men like to make notes before calling, and this isn't such a bad idea if you want subjects to kick things off, but don't stick to a script. Remember, most women love talking on the phone, so all you'll have to do a lot of the time is make a couple of leading remarks and let her talk to her heart's content. The first minute will seem like ten, but once you've both relaxed, and you will, it will become a lot easier.

Some men favour a short, terse conversation to arrange a time but I wouldn't recommend it, unless she feels really uncomfortable and you're able to sound confident and busy when you tell her you have to go. Instead keep it going as long as she's happy; women love the idea of a boyfriend they can have long phone conversations with, so if the pair of you can talk when you hardly even know each other, imagine what marathon conversations you might have in future, the sort that BT shareholders have wet dreams about.

Remember that for many women the phone is not just a functional business tool but also an extension of their very being.

How to leave a voicemail

If you're nervous this can seem like a blessing, or at least a stay of execution, but leaving an impressive message with a woman (or potential employer for that matter) can sometimes be hard.

Don't get flustered. One of the best scenes in *Swingers* – a film any student of pulling should watch – is when Jon Favreau's character, the one who's hopeless with the ladies, calls a woman whose number he got the night before. He doesn't like the message he leaves, so calls again to correct his mistake, gets flustered again and ends up leaving 16 messages. Unsurprisingly he doesn't get the girl.

So speak slowly and with a voice as deep as you can muster, say you're giving her a call to see how she is and to ask if she's free on a certain date, telling her to call you back at a specific time when you're not busy.

Text offenders

Never, ever ask a woman out by text; it's for cowards.

Dressing for a date

If you've already decided on the venue, there is only one thing you need worry about: what to wear.

'Men can make two mistakes when dressing for a date,' says Alison Tay, Style Editor of *Now* magazine. 'Trying too hard and not trying hard enough. On the one hand they go in for over-accessorising, overly matching, or anything attention-seeking. Or they come straight from the office, wearing ankle-skimming trousers and white socks; your corporate image will impress the boss but not your date. Wear a well cut, good-fitting, evening suit, and pay attention to the fit and quality. And wear pink! Any man who's confident enough to wear it is man enough to date.' For a pub date keep it simple, wear a vintage style T-shirt, your favourite jeans with something more casual, but always smart and clean.

And what about footwear? 'Wear a shoe-trainer hybrid for a posh restaurant. For a pub date, wear vintage low-tech trainers, something that's been around for years. Overdoing it says here's a man who spends more time on his appearance than you do, and no woman wants that.

'On the other hand, since women are obsessed with

their shoes, your date will probably be worrying about hers a lot more.'

Where to take her

Whatever you choose – cinema, restaurant, bar or something cultural – know what you want and don't leave it in her court. The important thing in dating is to do the work for her, otherwise it makes you seem as pathetic as a young boy tugging her skirt. A man with a grand plan in life should at the very least have a plan for Thursday evening.

You can make it a lot easier for yourself if you read a local listings magazine or website on a regular basis, to keep up with what club nights, exhibitions or new bars are opening. Women are far more interested in 'doing things' than blokes, who are often happy to sit in the pub and chew the fat.

Ask what interests her, and with your local knowledge offer to take her to something that sounds up her street. She might have been trying, to no avail, to get her friends to go to it, so she'd jump at the chance to go with you. The only risk with this strategy is that it's easier to get sucked into the friend zone, so you'll have to be doubly careful to act sexual when you meet up.

Back to yours

So you've had a great night, the conversation has flowed and you've managed not to bugger it all up by talking about *Robot Wars*. Now all you have to do is take her home. Simple, eh? There are a few things that may hold her back. Firstly, fear. You could be absolutely anyone as far as she's concerned, so make sure you don't push her. Make it clear that the offer is there for her to come back, and there are plenty of cabs available if she wants to leave.

Some men suggest using the ruse of 'I want to show you something,' in reference to an earlier conversation point about having a special signed CD or a massaging chair, but you don't want to look like you're tricking her. The best thing is to simply suggest coming back for a drink. Tell her you can't stay up too late, as you have to be up early in the morning, to relieve the pressure.

Also remind yourself that her staying over does not necessarily mean sex, because that will also be a fear. She might change her mind, or she might just want to cuddle. Think like that and you'll come across as being more honest and less predatory. But she's also scared of looking easy in her friends' eyes, and her own, so make an even greater effort to talk to her pals, and if you want, buy the guard dog another drink. If her pals like this new stranger talking to their friend, they're less likely to condemn her for going home with you. If the girls want to stick together, suggest her friend comes back too and sleeps on your very comfy sofa.

Girls also don't want to look like tarts in their own eyes, so never ever assume she's coming back to yours. Make it clear you'd like her to be there, but you understand if she doesn't want to – and that you'll survive either way.

And it's always useful to have some friendly cab

services ready to pick you up – nothing quenches the fires of passion like waiting half an hour for a tout to pick you up.

Your flat

Assuming you don't live with your mum, grandparents or a flatmate who's permanently glued to the sofa and stinks like a tramp, there are ways to turn an ordinary semi or bedsit into a veritable love nest, or at least a place where women won't scream when they first set foot in it.

Cleanliness

As a rule, women can't stand a messy environment. Right from the cradle, female babies are less tolerant of dirty nappies and cry more, while baby boys are happy to live in their own excrement; at the very least it prepares them for student life.

So in case any women are likely to pop round:

- Make sure the kitchen is clean, and that includes wiping the floor.

- Hoover all your rooms, especially the bedroom.

- Keep toilets and bathrooms clean; scrub the floor, put the seat down and, most of all, don't leave any evidence of piss on the floor or seat. It's amazing how many men still do this.

- Make sure the sink is free of shaving bits. Women find this disgusting.
- Have clean glasses and plates.

- And, of course, hide your collection of porn (and not under the bed, as trust me they always look).

Furniture

There's no need to deck it out like Austin Powers, but if you can, invest in a nice, comfy sofa. Women will want to lie with you by their side as they force you to watch the latest Jennifer Aniston movie.

Other must-have items:

- Nice lights – not too harsh. Install dimmers, if possible.

- Invest in some comfortable pillows, but not big, fluffy pink ones. She hasn't come for a slumber party, so don't overdo the femininity.

- Quality aftershaves and other products in the bathroom.

HOW TO PULL WOMEN

- Loads of candles, especially scented ones. Women love candles in themselves, but they also make the place smell a lot nicer.

- Have pictures of you and your mates on the wall, but not all pissing or mooning, and place pictures of attractive-looking women friends prominently. If she thinks they're your exes, you'll go up her in her estimation.

- Keep all the most female-friendly books and novels in a prominent place, and make sure your DVD shelf has the most intelligent and sophisticated t itles on display.

- If you're really suave, invest in a spare (unopened) toothbrush and give it as a gift.

17

The Morning After

Don't saw your arm off

If this is a one-night stand, there may be that awkward
moment when, depending on whose place you stayed
at, either she'll want to stay or you'll be desperate to get
out. (Then again, she may be just as keen to saw her
arm off to escape your embrace.)

Don't be horrible or gloating or fool yourself into
thinking she's a 'conquest', because that's the exact
opposite of a successful seducer's attitude. You should

be trying to make women happy, not just yourself, so don't let her leave feeling she's been used. And for that matter, make her breakfast while you're at it.

If it's just ships that pass in the night, but you have her number, then call her later or at the very least text, to make sure she's OK and doesn't feel cheap. She might regret what she's done and feel low, so do your best to make her feel better about it. That's because it's vitally important to end a relationship, however long, with the woman feeling good about you, not used and discarded.

The snowball effect

If one woman fancies you, others will follow, causing a very illogical snowball effect; for that reason don't be fooled into thinking that you should stay single because that will end in endless casual sex. Try dating, even if you don't think it will lead anywhere, as always having women around you will increase your market value. And who knows? One of them might even turn out to be the one, or at least the one before the one.

Treat her well, she will tell

There's an old saying; 'You meet everyone in life twice,' which translates as 'What goes around, comes around.' Treat women badly, and it will come back to haunt you, especially as they are far more open about comparing men to each other than we are. They might not discuss the finer details of sex, or at least I hope not, but if you're a scumbag, word will get out (there are even websites where women can dish the dirt on ex-boyfriends). But treat them well, and you'll have ex-lovers positively working as your personal press officer in future.

Stay on good terms

Though women like a bastard, falling out with an ex is a disaster. You might say there are plenty more fish in the sea, but she will poison the water supply. Always stay on good terms, and she might even recommend you to her friends.

Don't get a reputation as a liar, either as a cheating liar or just a bullshitter, as it's the worst image to have. Lying is also one of those counter-productive things we tend to do for a thrill, when it usually becomes more of an effort than simply being honest.

Be careful

Lust is a dangerous thing. It can get you beaten up, chained to a pregnant woman or make you suffer all sorts of awful metal probes in places you don't want them. You don't need another person lecturing you on being safe, but be careful in every way.

- Don't go home with a girl who is too drunk to make a decision, even if you're in the same state, as you're responsible by law.

- Don't come onto someone else's girl.

- Avoid any women who sets off your bunny-boiler radar.

- And don't let pulling rule your life. Create time for other things, and never let it get in the way of a friendship or do anything you wouldn't do if your genitals weren't doing the thinking.

And finally...

Despite a lot of evidence to the contrary, women don't want a bad guy; they don't want a gangster or a pimp, they want a fireman. In fact the best pulling tips will also make you a better person, so never be fooled into becoming nasty, selfish or bullying. Women want a man who has career goals, who looks after himself, who is kind to his family, who would help an old lady across the road, who has great friends and can stand up for himself and those he loves. Women want a good guy with balls.

Or on the other hand, you could always save up for that sports car...

Useful resources

Helpful guides

Street Magic, Paul Zenon (2005)
The Game, Neil Strauss (2005)
The Layguide, Tony Clink (2006)
Ask The Men's Health Girl Next Door , Nicole Beland (2003)
How to Get the Women You Desire into Bed, Ross Jeffries (1998)
How to Chat-Up Women, Stewart Ferris (2000)

Science

The Red Queen, Matt Ridley (2003)
The Mating Mind, Geoffrey Miller (2000)
The Selfish Gene, Richard Dawkins (2006)

Good websites

http://www.fastseduction.com
http://www.seduction.com
http://www.doubleyourdatingprogram.com
http://www.seductionexperts.com
http://www.seduction-and-dating.com
http://www.alphamalesystem.com
http://www.sirc.org/publik/flirt.html
http://www.datingclass.com
http://seducenow.com/neghits.html
http://askmen.com

Acknowledgements

Thanks to: Emma Grove, Jennifer Barclay, Steph Little, Catherine McQueen, Sophie Howard, Pete Cashmore, Paul Zenon, Hagop Tchaparian, Lia Emmerson, Alison Tay and all the men and women who offered sound, even if sometimes contradictory, advice.

MALE GROOMING

EVERY BLOKE'S GUIDE TO LOOKING GREAT

ED WEST

MALE GROOMING
Every Bloke's Guide to Looking Great

By Ed West

£4.99

ISBN: 1 84024 539 4
ISBN 13: 978 1 84024 539 4

Guys care more about their appearance than ever before. When we don't look good, we don't feel much better. Thankfully, though, looking sharp on the street is easier than you might think and the advice contained within from magazine journalist Ed West addresses everything you need to know about looking after yourself – from your hair to your toenails, and all the other stuff in between.

Ed West is the author of several humour books, and spent five years in the testosterone-charged offices of men's magazines before becoming a freelance writer. It was while working for *Nuts* magazine that he discovered a passion for moisturiser, hand cream and various other grooming products that only 20 years ago would have got him kicked to death by real men.

HOW TO CHAT-UP
BABES
Your place or mine?
You go to yours...
I'll go to mine.
STEWART FERRIS
summersdale humour

How to Chat-up Babes

By Stewart Ferris

£2.50

ISBN: 1 84024 368 6
ISBN 13: 978 1 84024 368 6

If your conversational techniques with women are more crassanova than Casanova then you need this little gem to improve your pulling power. Full of tips to boost your confidence with the opposite sex, no single bloke should enter a bar without this package tucked in his trousers.

- "Seduce her mind with the help of Stewart Ferris"
  Esquire

- "Hilarious book […] armed with this you can enchant her with your velvety wordplay"
  FHM

- "Learn how to talk to the opposite sex"
  Daily Mail, Weekend

- "offers some clear-headed advice plus a few giggles"
  Backpacker Magazine

Celebrity Chat-up Lines

CELEBRITY
CHAT-UP
LINES

STEWART FERRIS

Celebrity Chat-up Lines

By Stewart Ferris

£2.99

ISBN: 1 84024 368 6
ISBN 13: 978 1 84024 368 6

Just because they're rich, beautiful and successful doesn't mean that celebrities don't have trouble pulling. These are the chat-up lines they wish they could think of to have babes and blokes falling at their feet.

'The score between us is love all. How about we take it all the way to your advantage?'

Andy Murray

'Hi, I'm a prince. Let me take you back to my castle and show you the size of my turret.'

Prince Harry

Stewart Ferris was once voted one of the country's Most Eligible Bachelors (*Company* magazine) and was also nominated one of *Tatler* magazine's 200 best dates in town. He has appeared frequently on television as a flirting and dating expert.

www.summersdale.com